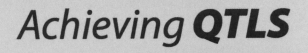

Teaching 14–19 Learners
in the Lifelong Learning Sector

Sheine Peart and Liz Atkins

LearningMatters

First published in 2011 by Learning Matters Ltd

British Library Cataloguing in Publication Data
A CIP record for this book is available from the British Library.

ISBN: 978 1 84445 365 8

This book is also available in the following ebook formats:
Adobe ebook ISBN: 9781844457632
EPUB ebook ISBN: 9781844457625
Kindle ISBN: 9780857250223

Cover design by Topics
Text design by Code 5
Project management by Deer Park Productions, Tavistock
Typeset by PDQ Typesetting Ltd, Newcastle under Lyme
Printed and bound in Britain by Bell & Bain Ltd, Glasgow

Learning Matters Ltd
20 Cathedral Yard
Exeter EX1 1HB
Tel: 01392 215560
info@learningmatters.co.uk
www.learningmatters.co.uk

Mixed Sources
Product group from well-managed
forests and other controlled sources
www.fsc.org   Cert no. TT-COC-002769
© 1996 Forest Stewardship Council

FSC

Contents

The authors

Sheine Peart is the academic team leader for Continuing Education at Nottingham Trent University, and lectures on Initial Teacher Education programmes for the lifelong learning sector. Before this she worked at South Nottingham College for 15 years, working on a variety of academic and vocational courses. She is a trained youth worker and has broad experience of practical classroom issues and extensive experience of working with learners who present challenging behaviour.

Liz Atkins spent 13 years managing and teaching on vocational programmes in FE colleges and also has extensive experience as an educator of teachers in the lifelong learning sector. Her published work focuses on in/equalities in education and the experience of students undertaking vocational programmes. She is currently Director of LLS Teacher Education programmes at Nottingham Trent University.

Acknowledgements

The authors would like to thank the Learning Matters Team for their continued support in producing this book; without their help this book would not have been written. In particular they would like to thank Clare Weaver for her ongoing guidance and patience and Amy Thornton and Julia Morris for their clear direction and vision.

1
Introduction

The purpose of this Introduction is to describe the structure of the book and explain why such a book is needed at this time. There is a long-standing debate in the UK between successive governments, educationalists and the wider population on the purpose and function of education, and a continuing dialogue between politicians, academics and practitioners on the education system needed to:

- satisfy the ever-changing needs of young people;
- meet the demands of industry and commerce;
- enable the UK to compete effectively in the global marketplace.

Education has played a key role in responding to these unfolding challenges and at times appears to have been viewed as a panacea, capable of solving all of society's problems. It is expected to raise the skills level of the nation, to solve social fragmentation and to produce a dynamic, economically vibrant and integrated society capable of meeting *all* future challenges. Central to meeting these challenges has been reforming the education system and, in particular, reorganising the structure and content of the 14–19 curriculum.

Why this book is needed

This book has been written for all teachers, tutors and trainers who work with 14–19-year-olds and anyone who has an interest in the education of this group of young people, whether they are in schools, in colleges, in employment or in work placements. Many of those who are now working with these young people have not followed traditional routes into education and are *drawn from industry, commerce and trades* (Wallace, 2010, page vii) and have been recruited into education because of their *valuable expertise in their vocational area* (ibid). Consequently, some tutors new to education have not had the opportunity to be involved in the educational debates as easily as those linked to education in more traditional ways. Additionally, the rapid pace of change means that even those who have worked in education and training for some duration have not had sufficient time to assimilate and process the quantity of information that has been produced by central government and other bodies.

This book is intended to address this information gap and to provide practitioners with the knowledge needed to understand the recent changes and, through a range of practical and reflective tasks, to equip tutors with the skills necessary to work effectively within the new 14–19 curriculum. Particular attention will be given to teaching Diploma courses and the challenges produced by these programmes.

The structure of the book and how to use it

This book has been structured to guide the reader through the principal issues relevant to the development and current organisation of the 14–19 curriculum, and each chapter deals with a different theme designed to extend your understanding of this subject. All chapters have been structured in a similar fashion. Each one begins by describing the chapter objectives and providing an outline of the chapter's focus, together with a list of the Professional Standards the chapter will help you to develop. All chapters provide a range of exercises, framed as reflective and practical tasks, to help you extend your understanding of the issues raised. Case studies are used to contextualise and locate the information given within a wider framework. References used within the chapter are provided at the end of each chapter, together with suggestions for further reading and useful websites to help you develop your knowledge further. If you choose, you can read the whole book from start to finish to gain a complete overview of the issues raised. Alternatively, you may prefer to read individual chapters that particularly interest you in your area of work. However, in order to derive maximum benefit, you should aim to attempt at least some of the tasks given within each chapter.

Chapters 2 and 3 provide a theoretical framework for the 14–19 agenda and trace the development of its origins and the current 14–19 agenda. Chapter 2 begins by providing a historical overview of the development of the 14–19 curriculum in the UK, exploring the tensions that have existed for successive governments reacting to growing public concern of a perceived 'dumbing down' of education and the lack of parity of esteem between academic and vocational qualifications. It describes how education has been structured according to age, rather than developmental stage, and the range of qualifications it has been possible for young people to achieve depending on whether they chose to study traditional academic courses or work-focused vocational programmes. It considers how these qualifications have often predetermined employment opportunities available for learners and how they sometimes became 'trapped' into narrow fields of employment, unable to accommodate a changing employment landscape.

This chapter also explores the demands of employers who have repeatedly indicated how the education system has failed to keep pace with industry and the consequent need for a more responsive, flexible system capable of meeting employers' requirements. It considers how these wide-ranging pressures produced a succession of government initiatives designed to bring coherence to the curriculum, allay fears from potentially confused learners and assure employers of the rigour and robustness of the qualification framework. However, with hindsight, many of these initiatives can now be seen to be flawed, produced as short-term 'quick fixes' more focused on political expediency, rather than the long-term needs of individuals, education, employers and the country. It can also be argued that such initiatives have failed to produce the long-requested coherent, easily understandable framework of qualifications, which clearly indicate the level and value of the various awards that can be studied.

Chapter 3 reviews the range of qualifications available for learners to study in more detail. It considers the value of these different qualifications and provides a tariff that allows the different qualifications to be compared against each other. It gives a detailed critical analysis of the 14–19 Diploma and debates the value of this qualification in comparison to the range of existing qualifications. It explores the range of short course accreditation available to learners and what function such qualifications serve for learners and for schools and colleges.

The following two chapters consider the more practical issues involved with teaching the 14–19 diploma and learners, alongside questions that may be raised as a consequence of working with this age range. Chapter 4 provides a timetable for the introduction of the Diploma, identifies the other qualifications that learners may choose to study and encourages you to review your own organisation's preparation for delivering the Diploma. It suggests strategies that may be useful when working with 14–19-year-olds and invites you to consider how appropriate these strategies are for the learners you teach. It directs you to actively debate the adequacy of your current learning environments and what steps colleges, schools and employers may need to take in order to prepare for delivering the Diploma. Concluding the chapter, it reviews the different opportunities for assessing learning and the challenges that assessing the Diploma, with its significant emphasis on work and employment, will produce for students and tutors alike.

Because the Diploma demands a different way of working with learners, Chapter 5 considers in detail the issues of working with 14–19-year-olds in colleges, and how to establish frameworks and environments to promote learning. It asks you to think how you can most effectively motivate younger students so that they wish to learn and make good choices when in a classroom environment. It directs you to review your role in this process and how your actions and behaviours may impact on learners' achievements. It considers what barriers may prevent learning, what role you may have in establishing or maintaining these barriers and how you can work to help deconstruct such obstacles. Finally, it reviews some of the tensions of having 14–16-year-olds on college premises, the significant difference between *loco parentis* and duty of care, and how colleges should prepare to accommodate learners in this age range.

Chapter 6 reviews the evolution of education communities and the advantages that can be gained by working in partnership with other organisations. It suggests types of working arrangements that colleges may wish to explore with schools or other partners and provides advice on how such collaborations might be managed, identifying potential areas of challenge. The chapter concludes with a review of the changing nature of college learners, the emergence of the NEET (Not in Education, Employment or Training) population, and how Every Child Matters (ECM) legislation now demands that all institutions working with young people, as well as having appropriate safeguarding procedures in place, take active steps to promote the five key aims of ECM.

The final chapter draws the arguments and debates raised in earlier chapters to a conclusion, linking the key themes and ideas identified together. However, this chapter recognises that the issues and discussions related to 14–19 education very much remain 'work in progress' and it is likely that further governments and academics will continue to debate these issues. To assist you in developing your understanding of this debate, it ends by identifying a range of further reading that you may find useful.

REFERENCES REFERENCES REFERENCES REFERENCES REFERENCES REFERENCES

Wallace, S (ed) (2010) *The Lifelong Learning Sector: Reflective Reader.* Exeter: Learning Matters.

2
Historical overview of 14–19 qualifications in the UK

The objectives of this chapter

This chapter aims to give you a historical overview of the 14–19 reform agenda. It is important to understand that the reforms did not just happen, and that many of the debates around the reform agenda, that we see in the education press and the wider media, have their roots in problems and discussions which, in some cases, can be traced back over hundreds of years. Therefore, this chapter explores a number of different aspects of 14–19 education, looking at the history and then relating this to the contemporary context.

This chapter provides support in helping you to achieve the following Professional Standards needed to gain QTLS status:

- **Equality, diversity, and inclusion in relation to learners, the workforce, and the community (AS3; AK3.1).**
- **Reflection and evaluation of their own practice and their continuing professional development as teachers (AS4).**
- **Understanding and keeping up to date with current knowledge in respect of own specialist area (CS1; CK1.1; CK1.2).**
- **Fulfilling the statutory responsibilities associated with own specialist area of teaching (CS3).**

Background to the 14–19 agenda

The contemporary 14–19 agenda, which has evolved over the past 20 years but increased in momentum during the 2000s as a result of initiatives implemented by the Labour government under Tony Blair and later Gordon Brown, seeks to provide a 'good' education for each young person which is appropriate to their needs and which will prepare them effectively for their future roles in the workplace. A key part of this policy since 2005 has been the development and implementation of the specialised Diploma. At the time of writing, the new Diploma qualification is in its second year of delivery, but it has an uncertain future: it has been subject to heavy criticism by teachers, academics and politicians. The Welsh government has chosen not to introduce it, but to implement a form of Baccalaureate (known as the Welsh bac), meaning that the Diploma only forms part of the qualifications framework in England. Announcements by the new Coalition government in June 2010 added to the uncertainty, with a reversal of the previous government's policy on a Diploma Entitlement. Instead,schools and colleges would be allowed to choose how many, and which, Diploma lines of learning they offered. Additionally, the decision to stop development of the Extended Diploma suggests that more extensive policy changes in 14–19 education may be announced, possibly in line with earlier Conservative party commitments to withdraw and replace the Diploma. However, constraints arising from the recession and the need to cut back public spending may also influence future political decisions and this can only add to the uncertainty surrounding the award. These political tensions about the future of this qualification reflect wider debates and disagreements about the 14–19 agenda and the different types of education (academic and vocational) that are, or should be, available to young people. These debates are also influenced by national economic and political pressures, such as the need to be able to compete economically in a global market or to combat youth unemployment, as well as by historical developments and debates around education.

Historically, many of the debates about the 14–19 agenda have their roots in arguments around parity of esteem. 'Parity of esteem' simply means that different types of qualifications and education are accorded the same respect and have similar outcomes in terms of the opportunities they offer. These debates have been with us for over a hundred years and reflect the socially divided education system in England and Wales and the very different social values placed on work which is done with the hands, and that which is done with the mind. This has resulted in similar judgements being placed on education that prepares for work with the mind, and that which prepares for work with the hands. In order to understand how the 14–19 agenda has evolved, and why it is the focus of such intense debate, it is necessary to look back and to consider some of the social and historical influences on education in England, as well as the intended and unintended impacts of policy over the past 20 years or so. This chapter will explore a range of interrelated issues, and place each of these in a historical context. The key issues include:

- the qualifications framework in England and Wales;
- historic and modern school-to-work transitions;
- the economic imperative for curriculum reform;
- the introduction of GNVQs and NVQs;
- the parity of esteem debate;
- the Tomlinson Review of 14–19 education; and
- the iGCSE and A* A level debates.

The structure of the qualifications framework in the UK

A tripartite system?

While much of the qualifications framework we are familiar with is of relatively recent construction, the 'gold standard' A level, around which it is built, is much older. Until 1951 a school certificate was available at 16+, although there were no credentials for those who left before this age. The minimum school leaving age in 1951 was 15: it had been raised from 14 in 1947 and was raised again to 16 in 1972. It has remained unchanged since that time, although changes first proposed by Alan Johnson (then Education Secretary) in 2006 and set out in the consultation paper *Raising Expectations: Enabling the System to Deliver*(2008), will require all young people, including those in employment, to be receiving approved education or training up to the age of 18.

The General Certificate of Education (GCE) at Ordinary (O) level, taken at 16+, and Advanced (A) level were introduced in 1951, replacing the School Certificate, and A levels subsequently became the entry qualification for university. At that time, however, only a tiny percentage of young people went into Higher Education (HE). A few undertook college courses (for example, a one year full-time course covering modern foreign languages as well as shorthand and typing was necessary to qualify as a secretary in the 1950s) or were apprenticed to skilled trades. A great majority moved into full- time, often unskilled, employment.

Since that time, many developments have taken place in education, including:

- significant increases in the numbers attending HE during the 1960s and 70s and beyond;
- the introduction of comprehensive education in the 1960s;
- the advent of 'new vocationalism' in the 1970s and 80s, ostensibly to address the issues of mass youth unemployment;
- the introduction of GNVQ and NVQ qualifications;
- multiple initiatives to end the so-called 'academic-vocational divide';
- the introduction of the Diploma and the Welsh bac.

These developments are contextualised later in this chapter, but have combined to give us a qualification (or credential) system which is dictated not only by age, but often by the type of secondary school or sixth form attended and the socio-economic status of the young person holding the particular credential.

Broadly speaking, at 14–19 there are three main educational 'pathways' that may be taken. Theoretically, these can be mixed and matched but, in practice, most young people tend to follow a single route. The three routes are academic (e.g. GCSEs and A levels); broad vocational (new Diploma and BTEC qualifications); and occupational (NVQs). In addition, the Foundation Learning Tier provides pathways to level 2 for learners working at Entry or level 1. While there is no Entry credential arising from GCSE (grades D–G equate to level 1), there are entry pathways on the Diploma and through the BTEC system, as well as a raft of other entry qualifications provided by Awarding Bodies such as National Open College Network (NOCN). Awards at the same level within these different pathways have had a notional equivalence attached to them for several years, and have recently been subsumed within a pan-European credit framework. This allocates different numbers of credits at different levels to approved qualifications in a system comparable to the Credit Accumulation and Transfer Points which has operated in HE for many years.

These three broad pathways or routes, together with alternative pre-level 1 provision, were confirmed in their present form in the DCSF Paper (2008b), which states that:

> *Learning for young people will lead to qualifications from one of four routes:*
>
> - *Apprenticeships – with an entitlement to a place by 2013 for all 16 year olds suitably qualified.*
> - *Diplomas – with an entitlement by 2013 for all 14–16 year olds to the first 14 Diplomas and for 16–18 year olds to all 17 Diplomas.*
> - *Foundation Learning Tier – with an entitlement by 2010 to study one of the progression pathways.*
> - *General Qualifications, e.g. GCSEs and A levels.*
>
> (DCSF, 2008b, p7)

This policy has a number of implications for 14–19 education. It reinforces the existing academic/vocational divide, which is deeply embedded in English education and is discussed in more depth later in this chapter. The curricula vary quite significantly in terms of content, mode of learning and types of assessment. This means that once established on a particular pathway, it can be very difficult for a young person to move to a different pathway. These difficulties are most apparent where young people wish to transfer from a vocational to an academic route and raise old questions about whether young people from particular backgrounds are being channelled into particular types of education and, later, particular types of occupation (Pring et al., 2009, page 117). In addition, from a pedagogic perspective, it also means that each of the pathways has a qualification-led (product-based) curriculum, which might lead us to ask fundamental questions such as whether this is the best way to educate young people or whether a curriculum more focused on process or praxis might be preferable.

REFLECTIVE TASK

Is the curriculum you deliver product- or process-based? How effectively does it prepare the young people for careers in your vocational sector? How might learning be improved? Would the changes you propose change the nature of the curriculum?

16+ qualifications

Traditionally, within this system, 16+ has been a key point, as it is (at the time of writing) the minimum school leaving age and the age at which most GCSE exams are taken. However, the government has tried, in recent years, to move away from the concept of GCSEs as a 'school-leaving certificate' and to encourage participation in and the achievement of post-GCSE credentials beyond 16. The 14–19 agenda, with its image of a seamless education throughout the phase, is a part of that initiative. Despite this, the qualifications system still provides for a 'break' at 16+, and in some cases at 17+ as well as 18+.

Programmes of study leading to national external examinations normally begin in Year 9, at age 14+. At this point, almost all young people are entered for core National Curriculum subjects at GCSE. Some young people will be entered for Diploma, BTEC or NVQ subjects at the same time. This is a controversial process. School league tables are largely based on numbers of passes at GCSE, and a vocational credential such as a Diploma is given a notional equivalence of a number of GCSE passes. This has led to suggestions that there is a temptation to enter some students, particularly those who are lower achieving, for vocational courses which have less credibility and which fix the young person on a particular educational pathway, in order to raise a school's place in the league tables. The opposite argument, put forward by the government, suggests that offering 'disengaged' young people an alternative curriculum, particularly where it is provided in an alternative setting, such as a college, can be highly motivating.

REFLECTIVE TASK

Think about the qualifications offered in your sector. What sort of income and career opportunities do they offer? Which of the two arguments above do you agree with? What are the reasons for your decision to support one rather than the other?

Outcomes and progression at 16+

The different qualifications young people are entered for at 14+ have significant differences in terms of outcomes and possible progression at 16+ (see Table 2.1).

Entry

Entry level qualifications include the Entry level Diploma and the BTEC Entry Level Certificate in Skills for Working Life. A young person gaining one of these credentials at 16+ would progress to alternative Entry provision or to level 1 provision such as BTEC Introductory Diploma or a level 1 Diploma.

Level 1

Level 1 qualifications include grades D–G at GCSE; level 1 Diploma; BTEC Introductory Diploma and NVQ level 1. Achievement of these credentials at 16 + may allow progression to GCSE resits (in some circumstances and at some schools/colleges); or to the level 2 Diploma; BTEC First Diploma or Certificate; NVQ level 2. However, only those young people with GCSE grades around the C/D borderline would progress to level 2 – those with grades at EFGU would be more likely to move on to a broad vocational level 1 programme.

Level 2

GCSEs at grades A*–C allows progression to any level 3 broad vocational programme; to level 2 NVQ or to A levels.
Level 2 Diploma allows progression to any level 3 broad vocational programme or to level 2 NVQ. Progression to A levels is possible but depends on the young person holding the right combination of GCSEs at C+ grades.

BTEC First: like the Diploma, this facilitates progression to level 3 broad vocational programmes or to level 2 NVQ. Again, progression to A levels is possible but depends on the young person holding the right combination of GCSEs at C+ grades.

Table 2.1: Qualifications by age and level.

Types of qualification

Beyond level 2, and at 16+, the situation becomes much more confusing. Some programmes are two years in length, but a significant minority of lower level broad vocational programmes are one year in length leading to a progression point at 17+. At 18+, progression from lower level broad vocational programmes is most likely to be either to higher level broad vocational programmes or into employment. Once in employment, the young people who have completed these qualifications may also be required to undertake additional, occupational training such as NVQs. From higher level broad vocational qualifications progression may either be into employment, where the requirement for occupational credentials will again arise, or into HE to a vocationally orientated programme. Young people on the NVQ route will typically be working towards level 2, but if they hold a senior position in their workplace, or are engaged in specific occupational areas (e.g. hair and beauty or childcare), this could be level 3. In many occupations level 2 is the minimum requirement for work in the trade, and this has implications for young people undertaking level 1 NVQ awards. For example, to gain employment as a plumber a young person would be required to hold a minimum NVQ level 2, although it is possible to undertake an NVQ level 1 in this area. Therefore, a young person holding a level 1 NVQ may only be able to access a trainee place. Those young people who have undertaken A levels will largely progress to HE, with the type of course and university dependent on A level subjects and the grades achieved. However, even these transitions are becoming less certain as a result of economic problems and more limited opportunities in the jobs market.

Clearly, this system is very messy. For most young people, and their parents, it is difficult to navigate and few people have an in-depth understanding of the nature of each credential and its potential outcomes in terms of occupational and life chances. However, the low take-up of the Diploma does suggest that many people are suspicious of this new qualification and this raises questions about how it will be accepted by employers and universities in the future. In 2008, 25 per cent of the expected numbers enrolled and although this rose in 2009, numbers still fell short of government predictions with less than 40,000 young people studying for a Diploma. This compares with 66,230 students undertaking an intermediate GNVQ in 2001/2002. The general confusion around different types of qualification also leads to young people applying for, or being placed on, the 'wrong' programmes, by which I mean those that will not lead to the outcome they desire. Sean and Emma are two examples given below, both of whom illustrate the need for clear guidance about the implications of different courses.

CASE STUDY

Sean and Emma

Sean applied to go to college shortly before sitting his GCSE exams. He was entered for nine subjects and expected to achieve at high grades. He attended an 11–16 school and wanted to become a doctor. No one in his family had attended university. Sean looked through the college prospectus and applied for a BTEC National in Health. He was unaware that for entry to medical school he required specific A levels at top grades and by the time he discovered this it was too late in the year to transfer to A level provision.

Emma wanted to be a nursery teacher. She had a difficult time during Year 10 when her parents divorced and underachieved in her nine GCSEs, gaining two D and seven E grades. Emma then progressed to college. Because she wanted to be a teacher but had low GCSE grades she was placed on a level 1 childcare course. Level 1 is not accepted as an occupational qualification in childcare where the minimum level to work under supervision is level 2. Many employers require level 3. Therefore, if Emma were to revise her ambitions to work as a nursery nurse, she would have to complete a further three years at college. If she persisted in her ambition to teach, she would have to move to an academic route which would enable her to achieve the GCSEs required for teaching before progressing through a route which enabled her to access and complete degree level education.

Both these case studies are 'real' people who have found themselves in the situations described and they show how difficult the system can be to navigate. This is partly because the system now demands that young people make decisions about their future at the age of 14 or soon after and, as we have seen, once a young person is established on a particular route it can be difficult to change direction. Again, this has significant implications for individuals, many of whom are not ready to make such momentous decisions so early in their career. For many young people, career decision making, career planning and navigating school-to-work transitions have all become increasingly uncertain in more recent times.

Discussion

If Sean and Emma were your students, what advice would you give them? What options do they have for the future? How could they most easily be supported to achieve their ambitions? How realistic are their ambitions? Which internal and external support agencies and mechanisms could you call on to help them?

School-to-work transitions: historic and modern

During the early to mid-twentieth century, school-to-work transitions were very straightforward and heavily differentiated by gender. Most young people left school at 15, later 16, and entered largely unskilled work. A smaller number were apprenticed (typically for seven years) to skilled crafts and trades, while fewest of all went to university and subsequently into the professions. These transitions were determined less by educational achievement, and more by social class and parental occupation. Hence, a skilled craftsman would use all the contacts and networks (or 'cultural capital') at his disposal to ensure that his sons had similar opportunities while a labourer would be aware of similar opportunities in his factory, and would use his influence, or capital, to try and obtain work for his children. Young women entered employment until such a time as they married and had children, but the occupations they went into were heavily gendered and very different to those of young men. For example, in steel-making areas such as Sheffield men would do the heavy and dangerous work in the casting of steel, while women known as the 'Buffer Girls' polished the fine cutlery produced by some of the works.

This situation remained largely unchanged up until the 1970s, except for an increase in the rates of young people moving on to university as a result of mounting numbers taking A levels, and the expansion of HE, which followed the Robbins Report published in 1963. However, by the 1970s the technological advances and industrial decline of the late twentieth century had combined to change the face of the jobs market in a way which would have been inconceivable a generation before, and led to the mass youth unemployment of the 1980s.

As a consequence of these events, a series of educational reforms, ostensibly intended to address problems of inequality, were pursued from the 1970s to the early 1980s and, over time, these reforms became known as 'new vocationalism'. The term 'new vocationalism' evolved within the context of mass youth unemployment as educational researchers began to distinguish between traditional vocational job *preparation* (as in an apprenticeship) and new initiatives ostensibly aimed at achieving job *readiness,* which emphasised the development of work skills such as punctuality and reliability. These initiatives came to be criticised as being *narrow and divisive* (McCulloch, 1987, page 32) forms of preparation for unemployment, rather than preparation for meaningful work (Bates *et al.*, 1984) and included programmes such as the Youth Opportunities Programme (YOP), Youth Training Scheme (YTS), Technical and Vocational Education Initiative (TVEI), and the Certificate in Pre-Vocational Education (CPVE). YOP provided pre-vocational preparation, while YTS had two pathways. The first involved employment (for the period of the scheme) with one day spent in college and the second pathway was a provision for those with learning difficulties and those considered not yet 'ready' for work. The scheme had no guarantee of a job at the end of it and the wages paid to those in employment were very low. The TVEI was a full-time programme for 14–18-year-olds, which combined general, technical and vocational education and included an element of work experience and was offered by schools and colleges. The CPVE was a one-year course for students aged over 16 in full-time education. It was intended to be a broadly based qualification that prepared students for either work or further vocational study.

The introduction of these initiatives led to a different type of transition for young people. The new transitions were less certain, and far more extended than in previous generations as young people undertook a range of low level vocational programmes in the hope that this would increase their 'employability' and, eventually, lead to some type of work. This situation became the focus of a major research project, known as the 16–19 ESRC project, during the 1980s. The project aimed to explore young people's transitions from school to the labour market, to establish how and why some trajectories were different and to understand the implications for individual young people's economic and political socialisation, self-concept and subsequent life chances (Roberts, 1993, page 229). It was a seminal piece of research that continues to influence thinking, writing and research around transitions and identity today. Much of that is concerned with how characteristics such as gender and social class influence identity and career choices, particularly in relation to vocational work. Early work arising from the project included that by Bates and Riseborough (1993), which explored the developing identities of the young people who participated in the study and that by Banks *et al.* (1991) who drew on the findings to explore how the adult occupational and political identities of the participants were established. Bates' work also informed later studies by Skeggs (1997), Colley *et al.* (2003) and Colley (2006), which all explore the development of identities appropriate to particular classed and gendered vocational occupations.

As a consequence of the ESRC 16–19 project, and the suggestion that came from it that some young people were being channelled towards predestined lives and occupations, ideas and writing around career routes and trajectories became very controversial (Roberts, 1993). These controversies persist in the debates and tensions around the 14–19 agenda and can be seen, for example, in the media brouhaha generated by the Tomlinson Committee proposal that A levels should be withdrawn.

Other work has examined the influences on transitions from school to work and career choice. Writing in 1996, Hodkinson *et al.* argued that all young people making transitions are influenced by 'Horizons for Action'. They suggest in their argument that young people make *pragmatically rational career choices* (page 3) constrained and enabled by external opportunities (such as the availability or non-availability of different types of work in the locality) and personal subjective perceptions (such as attributing a particular status or lack of status to an occupation, or having gendered ideas such as that young women should not become mechanics). In other words, young people make their decisions based on what they think is or is not an appropriate job for them and based on the opportunities available to them at that time and in that place.

Hodkinson (1996, pages 132–33) also proposed a theory, which he called *careership*. This theory rejected the concept of rational *ladder-like* trajectories where a young person takes GCSEs, progresses to level 3 credentials appropriate to the career they have chosen and then continues to progress through whatever levels of learning and development are necessary to achieve their goal. The theory of careership suggested that career developments or changes were based on turning points (for example, being made redundant or having a different kind of work opportunity presented unexpectedly – see case study below). Despite this, government policy today is based around the assumption that young people making the transition from school to work will 'progress' through a series of levels of education before making a straightforward transition into an occupation they have planned to enter since secondary school. However, in order to make a straightforward transition, young people need straightforward pathways. While the route from GCSE to A level and subsequently HE is straightforward, other pathways are less so, as illustrated in the case studies of Sean and Emma earlier in this chapter.

CASE STUDY
Natalie and Liam

Natalie left college with a Higher Diploma in Health and Society. She had always wanted to be a nurse, and had an offer from a local university. She intended to take a gap year and work before taking up her place. She got a job as a checkout assistant at a large supermarket. Natalie enjoyed her job and took all the in-house training courses on offer. Her section manager was impressed with her and mentioned this to HR and the store manager. Six months into her job, Natalie was offered a place on an in-house management training scheme. She accepted this, and did not take up her place at university.

Liam moved from GCSEs to a modern apprenticeship in plumbing, which he enjoyed. Unfortunately, due to the recession the company he worked for had to make a number of staff redundant, including Liam. He was part-way through his NVQ at the time. Liam applied for a lot of jobs, but was unsuccessful due to his young age and lack of formal qualifications. Eventually, after he had been unemployed for six months, his uncle, who worked in a warehouse, told him of a vacancy there. He was successful in getting the job, and pleased to be working again but, unlike the apprenticeship, this job was unskilled and offered no opportunity for progression.

The 2006 Nuffield Review identified a lack of clarity in some vocational pathways from level 3 to HE and the Working Group on 14–19 Reform (2003; 2004a; 2004b) found that there was a limited range of options at level 1. This suggests that the articulation of progression pathways is poor in many areas across all levels of vocational education, by which I mean that the progression through levels in some areas, or between areas, if a young person decides to change track, can be very difficult. These difficulties create structural barriers (which are absent for those young people following a more traditional transition from GCSE to A level and subsequently HE) that can be difficult to overcome, meaning that many young people find that they are unable to achieve their original career aims.

REFLECTIVE TASK

Identify the difficulties that face young people making a transition from school to work in the twenty-first century. Are these greater than they were for their parents or grandparents during the twentieth century? What are the differences? How can we effectively support young people to overcome the difficulties they face?

The needs of industry and employers – the economic imperative for curriculum reform

During the second half of the twentieth century, educational reform was increasingly influenced by, and later driven by, economic imperatives; a situation that remains unchanged today. In 1963, the National Committee of Inquiry into Higher Education (also known as the Robbins Committee) had been established. The first principle in its terms of reference stated that: *There should be maximum participation in initial higher education by young and* *mature students and in lifetime learning by adults, having regard to the needs of individuals, the nation and the future labour market.*This statement reflects an acknowledgement that economic success was related to the education of the working population and also makes an early reference to what we now know as 'lifelong learning'. The Robbins Report (1963), which arose from the work of this committee, identified a need for expansion in the HE sector to respond to the increased demand. Polytechnics emerged simultaneously to meet a perceived need for technological skill. It was hoped that this expansion would permit larger numbers of working-class teenagers to access higher education (McCulloch, 1994, page 34).

Until the 1960s, the vocational education and training followed by many young people had been largely independent of government control but significant changes took place during this decade. An increasing population led the government to establish the Carr Committee to investigate the apprenticeship system, and some of the changes in vocational education and training were directly related to its findings. There was also a recognition that the UK's slow rate of economic growth should be addressed and attempts were made to rationalise vocational education within a common framework (Raggatt and Williams, 1999, page 7). Together, these developments resulted in the establishment of the Business and Technical Certificate (BTEC) and of the Further Education Unit (FEU) in the 1970s, whose remit was to address the problems of the young unemployed and their need for further education.

Greater impetus was given to the development of vocational education by prime minister James Callaghan's speech of 1976, 'Towards a National Debate', which highlighted a number of social and economic issues facing the country at that time. This landmark speech, made at Ruskin College, Oxford, not only marks the date at which the so-called 'new vocationalism' policies originated, but also the point at which economic policy first became the 'driver' for education policy. The speech questioned the relevance to the world of work of much that was taught in schools. A range of initiatives designed to promote vocationalism within the school curriculum, including the TVEI and Young Enterprise, rapidly followed. Crombie-White (1997, page 197) later suggested that these initiatives ultimately led to the development of the National Framework for Vocational Qualifications. Their introduction was controversial; while some regarded them as innovative others were more critical. These opposing views were highlighted by Sikes and Taylor (1987, page 60) who argued that while official government discourse promoted the reforms as *liberating* there was a more critical view which saw them as *an invidious attempt to re-introduce the iniquities of occupational and even socio-cultural segregation.* Conversely, Weston *et al.* (1995, cited in Brooks, 1998, page 14) viewed the development in a positive light, suggesting that for young people with a history of low attainment the TVEI initiative improved attitudes towards, and participation in, post-16 education.

David Young, who with Norman Tebbit was one of the politicians most closely associated with the development of the TVEI initiative, believed that it was a major part of the answer to the youth unemployment of the time (Pring, 1995, page 63).This is significant as Millman and Weiner (1987, page 167) have argued that the introduction of TVEI was based on the belief that schools and education were partly responsible for the failure of many young people to find employment, something which is reflected in the fact that TVEI was created by the Department for Industry, rather than the Department of Education and Science (DES). Carr and Hartnett (1996, pages 162–63) have suggested that the implementation of these awards by the Conservatives, elected in 1979, formed part of a massive move towards centralisation of education.

Concerns about centralisation arose from the control over education and training that was exerted by the Manpower Services Commission (MSC). This government quango had considerable influence over the colleges via YTS, and over schools via TVEI (Gleeson, 1987, page 4). Although the MSC no longer exists, similar centralised control can be seen in the context of the National Curriculum for schools and, from 2001 to 2010, in the influence of the Learning and Skills Council (LSC) over the curriculum offered in colleges and other post-16 providers through a revised funding regime.

The LSC had been established following the White Paper *Learning to Succeed: A New Framework for Post-16 Learning* (DfEE, 1999). It subsumed the responsibilities of the old Further Education Funding Council (known as the FEFC, this was a funding and inspection body established eight years earlier following incorporation) for funding, while the FEFC's responsibility for inspecting the sector was transferred to OfSTED. Part of the LSC's wider responsibility was to *[work] with the pre-16 education sector to ensure coherence across all 14–19 education* (DfEE, 1999, page 7), a statement which effectively introduced into policy the concept of a 14–19 phase in education. The LSC was subsequently dissolved in 2010 following changes proposed in the consultation paper *Enabling the System to Deliver* (DCSF/DIUS, 2008), and funding for all 14–19 education returned to the local authorities (LAs), while responsibility for funding post-19 programmes moved to the Skills Funding Agency. In tandem with this, and as part of the 14–19 reforms, LAs also assumed responsibility for planning area-wide provision and ensuring that all young people are offered an 'entitlement', which includes Diplomas and Apprenticeships as well as GCSEs and A levels, although the commitment to an entitlement has since been withdrawn by the Coalition government. The changes announced by DCSF/DIUS owed much to the way policy initiatives were built upon two major reports into the FE sector, the first by Sir Norman Foster and the second by Lord Sandy Leitch.

The Foster Review and the Leitch Report

The Foster Review of the Further Education Sector, which reported in 2005, had the remit of advising on the 'key challenges and opportunities' facing FE colleges. The report found that FE colleges lacked what it termed a 'shared core purpose'. Foster believed that this could be resolved if the sector had:

> *an appetite to catch up with competitive international economies [and] a consequential core focus on skills and employability increasing the pool of employable people and sharing with other providers the role of enhancing business productivity.*
>
> (DfES, 2005b, page vii)

This emphasis on skills, which was accepted by the government, had many similarities with the emphasis of the Leitch Report, which followed a year later.

Sir Sandy Leitch had been commissioned to conduct a review of the country's long-term skill needs in 2004. It took two years to complete, and was published in 2006. As with the Foster Review, government immediately accepted its recommendations in the 2006 White Paper (DfES, 2006), since when it has had profound and ongoing implications for the FE sector.

Leitch placed great emphasis on *economically valuable skills*, to the extent of describing these as *our mantra* (DfES, 2006, page 2). He argued that the nation's skills and productivity lagged behind those of comparable economies and that this might undermine the UK's future prosperity. These concerns were tied to issues of social justice, and Leitch argued that improving skill levels could contribute to addressing existing social disparities in terms of income, child poverty and unemployment.

In order to achieve this, the report set out a series of skills-based objectives for the UK. These included the aspiration for the UK to become a world leader in skills benchmarked against the upper quartile of the Organisation for Economic Co-operation and Development (OECD) member states. Achieving the objectives by 2020, as recommended by Leitch, would involve *doubling attainment at most levels* and the targets set included:

- *95 per cent of adults to achieve the basic skills of functional literacy and numeracy, an increase from levels of 85 per cent literacy and 79 per cent numeracy in 2005;*
- *exceeding 90 per cent of adults qualified to at least level 2, an increase from 69 per cent in 2005. A commitment to go further and achieve 95 per cent as soon as possible;*
- *shifting the balance of intermediate skills from level 2 to level 3. Improving the esteem, quantity and quality of intermediate skills. This means 1.9 million additional level 3 attainments over the period and boosting the number of Apprentices to 500,000 a year;*
- *exceeding 40 per cent of adults qualified to level 4 and above, up from 29 per cent in 2005, with a commitment to continue progression.*

(Leitch Review of Skills, 2006, page 3)

These targets were underpinned by a series of principles, which included a focus on *demand led* and *economically valuable* skills. The review stated that *Skill developments must provide real returns for individuals, employers and society* and that they must *meet the needs of individuals and employers*. The report has had three key outcomes. Firstly, in response to the recommendation of the report that the skills agenda should be *de-politicised,* the Sector Skills Agency and National Employer Panel were merged to create the UK Commission for Employment and Skills (UKCES). UKCES provides advice on improving employment and skills systems to the four UK governments and gives employers a 'voice' in strategic and policy developments. Its five-year strategic plan (UKCES, 2009) sets out aims that are broadly similar to those in the Leitch Report. Secondly, the report resulted in significant changes of funding emphasis in the training of both young people and adults. While this has meant an increase in funding for the 14–19 age group, and for those with very low level or no credentials, there have been corresponding drops in funding for other groups, leading to a situation where adults wanting to improve their skills (or undertake educational, rather than skills-based courses) have been obliged to pay more for them than previously. This has led to concerns such as those raised by the National Institute of Adult and Continuing Education (NIACE) whose 2009 research found that the proportion of adults participating in learning was at its lowest level since Labour were elected. NIACE state that:

It is clear that a high price has been paid for the Government's skills strategy, and that the opportunity to gain a first qualification for a small cohort of the least qualified has been bought at the expense of engagement by large numbers of others from the same communities.

(NIACE, 2009, page 21)

These concerns reflect wider issues about equality and access to education, as well as acting as a reminder that whoever benefits from funding changes, there will always be someone who loses in a struggle for limited resources.

Leitch has also been a significant influence on the 14–19 agenda, informing many of the raft of initiatives which are still being implemented. These include policy initiatives such as those included in the 2006 consultation paper *Enabling the System to Deliver.* Examples of these include:

- the raising of the statutory school leaving age to 18;
- an entitlement to Diplomas, Apprenticeships and the Foundation Learning Tier for every young person;
- changes to A levels and GCSEs.

As may be seen from the discussion above, the 14–19 reform agenda is heavily influenced by the UK's perceived skills needs and, through bodies such as the Sector Skills Councils, the Sector Skills Development Agency and more recently UKCES, by the needs of employers. However, this approach to educational reform is not new. Many earlier initiatives such as TVEI were also influenced by economic, rather than educational imperatives, and other, later initiatives, including GNVQs, BTEC and particularly NVQs were constructed or influenced by groups of employers, giving them a significant voice in curriculum development.

PRACTICAL TASK PRACTICAL TASK PRACTICAL TASK PRACTICAL TASK PRACTICAL TASK

Find out how employers are involved in your vocational area. Discuss the contribution they make – is this in terms of advising on the qualifications framework or do they advise on, and perhaps commission specific courses tailored to the needs of their employees? What is your personal contribution to meeting the needs of the employers? Do the needs of the employers and the needs of the learners ever conflict?

Vocational qualifications, apprenticeships and parity of esteem

In 1986, under the Conservative government of Margaret Thatcher, the joint MSC & DES report *Review of Vocational Qualifications in England and Wales* identified five major concerns with relation to vocational qualifications in England and Wales. These included *the unhelpful divide between so-called academic and so-called vocational qualifications* which *should be bridged*, also identifying that *there is no national system for vocational qualifications* (1986, page 1). This report gave birth to NVQs, now established across almost all vocational areas. Considered innovative at the time of their inception, NVQs are 'competence-based' qualifications, and their intention was to provide employees with the opportunity to demonstrate their competence in the job they were already doing. However, they rapidly also evolved into occupational training courses offered first by FE colleges and later, as the sector became more diverse, by employers and private training providers. More significantly perhaps, their introduction was the point at which the emphasis of occupational training changed from being input driven to being assessment driven (Wallace, 2008, page 198). Since these early days, only NVQ qualified assessors have been able to assess NVQ awards. To meet these criteria, the assessors have to both be occupationally competent in their vocational field and hold the relevant NVQ Assessor Units, originally called D Units and later A Units.

The competence-based framework requires candidates to demonstrate, by the submission of assessed evidence, usually in the form of a portfolio, their competence against standardised, nationally approved performance criteria and knowledge specifications, which were developed by 'lead bodies' consisting of employer representatives from a particular sector. Following the introduction of the award candidates were able to work towards a qualification without attending a programme of study and could be given Accreditation of Prior Experience and Learning, which was intended to make the qualification much more accessible, supporting the government aim of creating a much more highly qualified workforce. However, concerns about standards and quality resulted in the reduction of the qualification to minutely detailed performance criteria which were criticised as making NVQs *highly fragmented, almost incomprehensible, qualifications* (Smithers, 1997, page 56). The awards have been revised in response to these and similar criticisms and are now much simplified, but corresponding concerns about quality persist.

More recently, Hodgson *et al.* (2007, page 326) citing work by Keep (2004) have argued that the narrow nature of NVQ qualifications does not encourage the development of wider skills for life and that in many low-skilled areas there is a lack of a progressive career structure and reward for improving one's qualifications. Brockmann *et al.* (2008, page 227) in a comparison of the French and English *VET* (Vocational Education and Training) systems argue that, in England, competence refers to the performance of fragmented and narrowly defined tasks, with minimal underpinning knowledge and usually denotes functional employability for what may be relatively low-skilled employment. This view is generally supported by the fact that although NVQs were intended to provide a route to HE as well as the workplace, this route was never really established. They remain largely an occupational qualification, with most awards gained being at levels 2 and 3 despite the availability, in a small number of occupational areas, of awards at levels 4 and 5 which reflect significant managerial expertise and, according to the NQF, equate to postgraduate levels of attainment.

Modern Apprenticeships

NVQs have, however, formed the basis of the Modern Apprenticeship system, which has developed over the past 15 years. Apprenticeships were the principal form of work-based training up until the 1970s and the advent of new vocationalism. The work-based training routes followed during the 1980s were mainly the now discredited government-sponsored schemes such as YTS and YOP. Apprenticeships re-emerged in the form of the Modern Apprenticeship in 1994. Successive governments were committed to making them a high quality option, comparable to schemes in Europe, but progress in working towards this was slow. Initially this was partly due to a localised funding methodology, which meant that there were wide variations in the funds allocated to Modern Apprenticeships. Comparisons were also inevitably made with the YOP and YTS schemes. As recently as 2003, Fuller and Unwin noted that the Modern Apprenticeship has *struggled to meet expectations and in many occupational sectors, apprentices leave without completing the prescribed qualifications* (page 5). They went on to argue that one reason for this was that the government was more concerned with using the route to promote social inclusion than in developing high quality work-based training.

Today, there is still considerable variation in the quality of different Modern Apprenticeships. Some apprentices are provided with extensive training and, once qualified, have good career opportunities in their field or organisation. Others have poorer quality training and fewer opportunities. Despite these inequities, and the difficulties associated with developing a high quality national system, the Labour government pursued the Apprenticeship model post-16 and, in 2005, announced the introduction of Young Apprenticeships for 14-year-olds as part of the 14–19 reforms. These reforms also made work-related learning a statutory requirement. Later policy developments introduced an entitlement to an apprenticeship place by 2013 for all 'suitably qualified' 16-year-olds (DCSF, 2008, page 7).

GNVQs

The GNVQ was first introduced in 1992, rapidly following the introduction of the NVQ. Initially, only level 2 and level 3 awards (later to be renamed Intermediate and Advanced) were introduced; however, they were followed in 1993 by the introduction of the level 1 (later Foundation) GNVQ, although this was only ever available in a very limited number of subjects. In common with the NVQ, the award was build around nationally approved and standardised criteria. Assessment was mainly by coursework, but included multi-choice examinations in core units.

The introduction of the GNVQ award framework arose from the White Paper *Education and Training for the 21st Century* (DES, 1991) and formed part of a strategy to increase participation and achievement in post-compulsory education and training (Bathmaker, 2001, page 83), although they were also offered in schools from very early in their lifetime. In 2002, the Green Paper *14–19 Extending Opportunities, Raising Standards* proposed that all 6-unit GNVQ qualifications (i.e. level 1 and level 2) should be withdrawn and replaced by Applied GCSEs (previously Vocational GCSEs or VGCSEs), with a Foundation (level 1) qualification being equivalent to D–G grade and an Intermediate (level 2) equivalent to C+. Post-Compulsory Education and Training (PCET) professionals made urgent representations to government over this change. In their view, a tried and tested formula such as GNVQ was much better than moving young people down a GCSE route when their very presence on low level programmes indicated that they had already 'failed' at GCSE – entering such students for a qualification with the same name as the one they had 'failed' was likely to be demotivating. These representations resulted in a policy compromise on the issue, and the subsequent White Paper decreed that both 6-unit GNVQs and Applied GCSEs should continue to operate until *suitable alternatives* (to GNVQ) were available (DfES, 2003a, page 25). The 6-unit awards were finally withdrawn in 2007, the Advanced award having been replaced earlier by the short-lived AVCE as part of the Curriculum 2000 initiative. BTEC qualifications at different levels, and level 2 and 3 Diplomas are the successor qualifications to GNVQ.

The introduction of the GNVQ in the early 1990s built on the earlier initiatives of TVEI and CPVE and both this, and subsequent vocational initiatives such as AVCE, VGCSE and the Diploma may be considered to have their roots in the new vocationalism of the 1980s. The GNVQ created considerable interest in academic circles and it was the focus of extensive research activity throughout its life. However, this focused almost exclusively on the Advanced qualification and as a consequence, the level 2 (intermediate) award received little critical or academic attention and the foundation (level 1) almost none at all. The substantial body of work around the GNVQ has explored a range of issues. Two of the most important aspects of the research are the debates around parity of esteem and broad criticisms of vocationalism, which were generated by the introduction of the GNVQ awards. Essentially, critics of the award suggested that new vocational programmes such as GNVQ were preparing young people for particular roles in the workplace, and that these roles were lower paid, lower skilled and held in lower esteem than those that might be accessed through the academic route.

Debates that began with the advent of new vocationalism were developed and informed later work on the GNVQ. Some of these have subsequently been applied to successor qualifications of the GNVQ such as the Diploma. It is possible to trace these arguments through literature over time. For example, in 1984 Clarke and Willis criticised the early vocational initiatives and argued that a perception that young people need to be inculcated not only with the skills, but also with the right *attitudes* for work had its origins in Callaghan's Great Debate about education (1984, page 3). They went on to discuss how this perception was justified in the context of the mass youth unemployment of the time. Also writing in 1984, Moore extended this argument, suggesting that there was a related view that those young people who *required* (author's emphasis) inculcation with the right attitudes and skills for work belonged to a particular category of non-academic low achievers. He went on to argue that this view assumed a *deficit model* for these young people (1984, page 66). A deficit model is one where the focus of a problem is seen to be the student, rather than the institution or social or educational structures in which they are located. This notion of a deficit model has also been used by more contemporary writers discussing young people on vocational programmes (e.g. Atkins, 2009, page 6) while Unwin has argued that VET generally is *...deficit activity, reluctantly funded by government* (2004, page 147). Other more recent work has suggested that the inculcation of particular skills and attitudes effectively prepares young people for specific, low pay, low skill occupations (Ainley, 1991, page 103; Helsby *et al.*, 1998, page 74; Bathmaker, 2001, page 85; Ecclestone, 2002, pages 17–19).

These arguments are important because they suggest that programmes such as the GNVQ and its successors lead to a form of pre-ordained positioning within the labour market, ultimately determining the future life chances of the individual and so contribute to the replication of social class in future generations. If this is indeed the case, then that suggests that achieving parity of esteem between qualifications of different types may not be possible, despite the multitude of government initiatives which have sought to achieve it. If such a situation were accepted, it would demand a completely different approach both to education policy and curriculum development.

Parity of esteem

Many of the initiatives introducing vocational qualifications have sought to create a greater parity of esteem, or equality, particularly between A levels and alternative level 3 qualifications such as NVQ level 3, level 3 Diploma, BTEC Nationals and latterly the GNVQ Advanced. However, arguments about parity of esteem in education in England and Wales date back well over 100 years, and have their origins in the different societal esteem placed on different types of occupation and the different types of preparation for those occupations. Since a person's occupation and education are largely determined by their social class, or that of their parents, these debates and issues in education are indivisible from concerns about the rigid and highly stratified social class system which exists in England and Wales.

The tensions between the academic and vocational curriculum, and their relationship to social class, were first noted as long ago as the Taunton Report of 1868. This identified three different types of secondary education according to the social class of the child's parents: those in the first class would expect an education to the age of 18 or beyond, before entry to business or the professions, and focused on the liberal (or classical) curriculum, which involved the study of the classics and the Latin and ancient Greek languages. The second type of education, expected to last up to the age of 16, was more broadly based including subjects such as mathematics, and met the demands of the *wealthier part of the community*. Finally, a basic education covering reading, writing and arithmetic was available to the lower middle classes (see McCulloch 1998, pages 12–16). In this way, distinctions were made between the different types of education considered appropriate to children from different social classes (although, as you may have noticed, no mention was made of working-class children!).

Class divisions based on what was considered 'fit' for people from different strata of society have remained firmly entrenched within the education system, and continue to be the source of much discussion (McCulloch, 1994, page 60; Woodward, 2002, page 3). They were clearly reflected in the Bryce Report (1895), which recommended a grade of secondary education for working-class children;the Spens (1938) and Norwood (1943) Reports; and in the tripartite system established by the 1944 Education Act, which accepted the recommendations of the Norwood Report. This established Grammar, Secondary Technical and Secondary Modern schools for children with *different types of mind*. Norwood described the young people who would go to Grammar schools as *interested in learning for its own sake, ... can grasp an argument or follow a piece of connected reasonin*g, while the young person most likely to receive a technical education *often has an uncanny insight into the intricacies of mechanism whereas the subtleties of language construction are too delicate for him* and finally, those pupils who *deal more easily with concrete things than with ideas* (1943, pages 1–3) would receive a secondary modern education. Few secondary technical schools were built in the struggle for post-war reconstruction, meaning that while a few children were able to access a traditional Grammar education most attended secondary modern schools, which offered far fewer opportunities in terms of education, progression and future possibilities. The tripartite system is often referred to as Platonic, because it is modelled on the ideal education, which Plato propounded in his book *The Republic*. Plato believed that different types of education should be available to different types of child. He split these different types of child into three groups according to the social structures of ancient Greece, and described the education each would need according to his station in life: Plato refers to these three groups and types of education as gold, silver and copper.

Education policy during the 1990s and 2000s established three separate educational routes of NVQs, Diplomas and similar broad vocational qualifications (such as BTEC and latterly GNVQ) and A levels and GCSEs within what became a 14–19 framework. This process began with the 1991 White Paper *Education and Training for the 21st Century*. As a result of the wide-ranging policy developments outlined in this paper, FE colleges were incorporated (making them independent institutions and releasing them from LA control) *and the three-track qualifications pathway outlined earlier in this chapter was introduced.* The paper acknowledged the divide between academic and vocational qualifications, resulting in a lack of esteem for vocational qualifications and asserted the government's intention to achieve parity of esteem for all types of qualification by the introduction of *mixed programmes of learning* in which young people would combine a range of academic and vocational qualifications according to their needs and abilities (DES, 1991).

The paper identified three clearly differentiated pathways that young people could follow.

- National Vocational Qualification (NVQ) or craft paths.
- The vocationally slanted, but more theoretical, college-based General National Vocational Qualifications (GNVQs).
- The academic A and AS levels (DES, 1991, page 18).

These pathways were confirmed by the final report of the Dearing Committee (1996, page 13). The system has been described as the *new tripartite* (McCulloch, 1995, page 128) and clearly echoes the Norwood Committee's description of *different types of mind* with class divisions evident in the new three-track (tripartite) system. Broadly speaking, within the current system, the A level track tends to be followed by middle-class children who use it to access HE and well-paid, professional employment. The broad vocational alternative (BTEC National; Specialised Diploma) tends to be followed by students from slightly lower socio-economic groups. These qualifications will access some HE provision, but not all, and are likely to lead to employment in technical, vocational and lower status professional occupations, which may be less secure and lower paid than the more highly esteemed professions, such as law or medicine, accessed through the A level route. The NVQ route offers a qualification in a lower paid occupation, often with little or no opportunity to progress (Keep, 2004). These debates have persisted with the introduction of the Diploma, which, it has been suggested, merely fills the *middle track* vacated by GNVQs and which has failed in the past (*Enabling the System to Deliver*, DCSF/DIUS, 2008). Clearly, a much more radical approach is necessary if parity of esteem is to be achieved. Fifty years ago Dr Olive Banks made such a radical suggestion, arguing that parity of esteem cannot be achieved without a wholesale change in social values (McCulloch, 1995, page 125).

Writing in 1997, Spours argued that historical problems could be addressed by a unifying reform policy which addressed the academic/vocational divide, such as that proposed by the 1991 White Paper of overarching diplomas at ordinary and higher level (1997, page 72). This was a prescient statement in the light of his future role as a member of the Working Group on 14–19 Reform, which recommended curriculum reform along similar lines. Most commentators, however, consider that the issues are too deep-rooted to be overcome. McCulloch (1995, page 129) argues that it is unlikely that the concept of parity of esteem can overcome the historical and cultural differences between the different forms of education and Robinson (1997) describes parity of esteem as 'a myth', suggesting that there can be no parity of esteem in education because there is no parity of esteem in the labour market. Further, the students in a 2001 study conducted by Bathmaker were quite clear that, whatever the arguments around parity of esteem, the GNVQ was a lower status qualification (2001, pages 94–5), and others have made similar arguments.

A plethora of government initiatives in recent years has sought to address the issue. It is possible to argue that their failure is, at least in part, due to a perception among policy-makers that it is vocational qualifications which are in need of change, and this leads to a particular policy approach. For example, parity of esteem formed the main focus of the 2002 Green Paper *14–19: Extending Opportunities, Raising Standards.* This paper inferred that to have parity with one another, qualifications should have equal *academic rigour*. However, it is possible to argue that although some level of academic skill is necessary to achieve most qualifications, in trying to achieve parity of esteem through academic rigour we prevent it occurring. This is because the emphasis on academic rigour immediately establishes this concept, rather than vocational or technical skill, as the most important. Similarly, the 2005 White Paper which gave birth to the Diploma and the 2008 DCSF paper which confirmed the different educational routes both emphasised the vocational, while retaining A levels and GCSEs against the advice of the Tomlinson Committee. Therefore, both may be seen to be trying to address perceived problems with vocational education, rather than addressing inequalities within the system as a whole. These issues have formed a focus for concern for the Nuffield Review of 14–19 education. Returning to more radical suggestions for addressing issues of parity of esteem the authors of a book arising from the review make the following argument:

> *Perhaps the search for parity of esteem which lay behind these and so many other changes is not so much a false as a meaningless aim. There are different kinds of learning experience, different kinds of courses. [We] argue that, rather than pursue parity of esteem in a highly divided system (with all the fabricated equivalences which that entails) the basic structure of the qualifications system has to be addressed. We argue for a more unified approach in which different pathways can be pursued, each pathway justified in terms of the quality of learning and employment opened up.*

(Pring *et al.*, 2009, pages 7–8)

Pring *et al.* go on to argue for a baccalaureate structure with a common core and the chance to specialise; a development of the proposals which arose from the deliberations of the Working Group on 14–19 Reform, better known as the Tomlinson Committee.

REFLECTIVE TASK

To what extent is there parity of esteem in your vocational area? Are there clear pathways leading to employment and/or HE? What are the likely occupations and income levels of your students when they have moved into work? How well respected are these occupations by society? How do they compare with careers accessed through the traditional A level and HE route?

The Tomlinson Review of Education

The remit of what has become called the Tomlinson Committee was to *develop proposals for major reform of the curriculum and qualifications in England for young people aged approximately 14–19* (Working Group on 14–19 Reform, 2003, page 1). Much of the emphasis of the committee's work was to make recommendations for a new system of post-14 credentials, which would provide for the needs of all young people, and consign the debates around parity of esteem to the history books.

The Tomlinson Committee was established following widespread concern about examination standards, which arose from discrepancies in A level marking in 2002. These concerns broadened and eventually came to involve the more popular sections of the national media, rather than just being confined to the academic press. The controversy became the focus of major headlines such as *Six weeks to re-think A-Level marking* (*the Guardian*, 14 October 2002) and *Exam crisis: 'Heads will roll' if results were manipulated* (*The Independent*, 20 September 2002).

Inevitably, this led to pressure on the government and, eventually, the resignation of Estelle Morris who was Education Secretary at the time, as well as the dismissal of the head of the Qualifications and Curriculum Authority (QCA), a regulatory and development quango, which was subsequently restructured under a different name. The establishment of the Working Group formed part of the government response to these events.

The Working Group undertook a wide-ranging consultation with public and education professionals and published a number of papers during this time. The final report was published in October 2004 and endorsed a baccalaureate-type system. The creation of a new qualifications system from entry level to level 3 within an overarching Diploma was proposed. The new system was designed to facilitate movement between different tracks or pathways, and the committee intended that it would eventually replace all existing qualifications at levels 2 and 3 of the National Qualifications Framework. The ideas they presented were not new: Ken Spours and Ann Hodgson, both of whom served on the Working Group, are among a number of academics who had been advocating the introduction of a baccalaureate or diploma system for a number of years.

The Diploma framework recommended by the Working Group included what was described as core and main learning. Core learning included functional literacy and communication, functional maths and ICT. In addition, the core learning part of the Diploma would introduce another innovation – the extended project, which all young people would undertake and which would allow them to investigate a subject of interest to them at a level equivalent to the Diploma they were undertaking. Statutory National Curriculum requirements for Key Stage 3 would be retained as a basis for core learning. Main learning would be undertaken in subjects chosen by the learner to develop *knowledge, skills and understanding of academic and vocational subjects and disciplines which provide a basis for work-based training, higher education and employment* (Working Group on 14–19 Reform, 2004b, page 5). Together, these and other innovations were intended to raise participation and achievement, improve functional skills, strengthen vocational pathways, provide more stretch and challenge and create more coherent pathways of learning.

Despite receiving widespread support from the education sector, the recommendations of the Working Group were criticised both for retaining a broad triple-track approach, which, similarly to the existing system, encompassed academic, vocational and occupational study and for proposing the abolition of 'gold standard' A level and GCSE credentials. Once again, much of this criticism appeared in the popular media and many of the more radical proposals were rejected by a Labour government which was facing a third general election in May 2004 and feared the electoral implications of dismantling A levels and GCSEs. Instead, the government rushed out the White Paper *14–19 Education and Skills* in February 2005, which retained A levels and GCSEs, subject to a review in 2013, and introduced the 'specialised' Diploma, now just the Diploma, across six vocational areas (known as 'lines'). The government plans to increase these to 17 lines by 2011. The White Paper also introduced the general (GCSE) Diploma which is based on 5+ GCSEs at grades A*–C including maths and English. The government has suggested that A levels will be marginalised by the Diploma as take-up improves, but this is open to question, particularly given the extent of the criticism of these reforms.

The iGCSE and A* A level debate

Part of the government proposals in the wake of the Tomlinson Review were to ensure the rigour of GCSEs and A levels in the face of criticism that they were being 'dumbed down' and getting easier. These criticisms were largely drawn from the independent schools sector and from elite state schools, which recorded high pass rates at high grades at both GCSE and A level, as well as from media pundits. Within the independent sector, which operates free of many of the curriculum constraints imposed on the state sector, many schools have chosen to offer the International GCSE (iGCSE) in response to these concerns. The iGCSE is offered in International schools across the world and has had comparisons drawn with the old O level exams because it is examined largely by terminal exam and is therefore perceived to be more rigorous. A comparison of the GCSE and iGCSE by QCA found that *the iGCSE cannot be regarded as assessing the relevant programme of study to the extent that the GCSE does* (QCA, 2006, page 12). Essentially, they argued, the iGCSE did not meet National Curriculum requirements for Key Stage 4.

An earlier study by Dexter and Massey (2000, cited Bell and Dexter, 2002) found that *IGCSEs' grading standards are well in line with those pertaining in GCSE examinations across the range of disciplines,* but they too drew attention to differences in the syllabus within the same subject area, suggesting that in comparing the exams for, say, English GCSE and English iGCSE we are simply comparing apples with pears: the exams do not bear comparison in terms of content. Despite this, pressure continued for state schools to be allowed to teach and examine the iGCSE syllabus while the Labour government insisted that they retain standard GCSEs. As a result, the issue has received considerable coverage in the wider media as well as the Education press. Headlines have included *DCSF refuses to fund IGCSE core subjects in state schools* (*Times Educational Supplement,* 6 November 2009), *IGCSE row as state schools are banned from offering 'rigorous' exams* (*Daily Telegraph,* 4 December 2009) and *Teenagers secretly taking 'O' Levels because GCSEs are 'too easy'* (*Daily Mail,* 5 December 2009). The Coalition government has announced since the election in May 2010 that schools will be able to choose the qualifications they want their pupils to take, signalling a lessening of central control over the curriculum. However, the arguments around dumbing down of the curriculum persist, with particular concerns around science and maths at GCSE, and can be guaranteed to make headlines during August each year, when GCSE and A level results are published.

Much of the criticism about the alleged dumbing down of A levels has been based on statistics over the past quarter of a century, showing year-on-year increases in the pass rates. By 2009, 97.5 per cent of all entries passed and 26.7 per cent of these were A grades. Inevitably, this creates problems for universities, particularly those prestigious institutions offering high status programmes for which the standard entry is 3 A grades at A level. These institutions have lobbied hard for a revised system that will allow them to more easily identify the most able students from among the increasing numbers with 3 A grades. The new system establishes an A* grade at A level for the first time. This was announced following a review of A levels in 2005 and introduced with a number of other changes in 2008. It builds on a recognition in the *14–19 Education and Skills* White Paper that there was a greater need for differentiation amongst the increasing numbers of young people achieving straight A grades at A level (DfES 2005a, page 64), and replaces the Advanced Extension Award which some schools were using for differentiation purposes. In order to achieve an A* a student must achieve a grade A overall at A level and also achieve 90 per cent or more on the uniform mark scale (UMS) across their A2 units. The A* grade was first awarded in August 2010, and carries an additional 20 UCAS points to a standard A grade. As with other reforms, this one has had a mixed reception.

It can be argued that by strengthening the A level in this way, the qualification has become even more elite, and that this will weaken vocational routes further. However, the A* A level has been welcomed by those universities considered to be amongst the most prestigious. For example, the University of Cambridge website states that:

Cambridge welcomes the introduction of the new A* grade at A level ... Analysis of our current students' achievement suggests that the vast majority would have been awarded at least one A* had the grade been available when they took A levels. In light of this the standard A level conditional offer made by the Cambridge Colleges for 2010 entry will be A*AA.

(University of Cambridge, 2009)

No doubt the debate will continue, and it is likely to draw extensive press coverage each time the A level results are published in August, particularly in the early years of the new grade.

A SUMMARY OF **KEY POINTS**

These developments laid the foundation for the development of the 14–19 agenda we know today. This agenda includes a whole raft of reforms introduced over the past few years, which, despite their intention to improve educational opportunities for young people and prepare them more effectively for the globalised workplace cannot be detached from their historical context, and, like their predecessors. They remain mired in controversy, and have been the cause of a multitude of initiatives visited on 14–19 teachers during the past few years. Pring *et al.* (2009, page 191) have stated that *teachers and college lecturers feel as if they are on the receiving end of endless change.*

Ultimately, what all this tells us is that the contemporary 14–19 agenda is a product of its history, and of the economic and political expectations placed on it. This means that, particularly early in the life of a new government, it will continue to be subject to policy changes and initiatives. Understanding what has gone before, particularly since the advent of new vocationalism, will help you to understand the changes in this dynamic sector as they occur, and enable you to critically reflect on professional issues such as those around inclusion, equality, parity or the implementation of new initiatives.

This chapter has explored:

> the structure of the qualifications framework in the UK as determined by age and type of qualification;

> the introduction of GNVQs/NVQs and other vocational qualifications;

> parity of esteem between academic and vocational qualifications (A levels/GCSEs v BTECs and other vocational qualifications), including the (re-) emergence of work-based training routes including apprenticeships;

> school-to-work transitions – historic and modern;

> the needs of industry and employers – the economic imperative for curriculum reform;

> the Tomlinson Review of Education;

> the iGCSE and A* A level debate.

REFERENCES REFERENCES REFERENCES REFERENCES REFERENCES REFERENCES

Ainley, P (1991) Education for Work, in Chitty, C (ed) *Changing the Future.* London: The Tufnell Press.

Atkins, L (2009) *Invisible Students, Impossible Dreams: Experiencing Vocational Education 14–19.* Stoke on Trent: Trentham Books.

Banks, M, Bates, I, Breakwell, G, Bynner, J, Emler, N, Jamieson, L and Roberts, K (1991) *Careers and Identities.* Buckingham: Open University Press.

Bates, I and Riseborough, G (eds) (1993) *Youth and Inequality.* Buckingham: Open University Press.

Bates, et al. (1984) *Schooling for the Dole?: the New Vocationalism.* Basingstoke: Macmillan Publishers Ltd.

Bathmaker, A-M (2001) 'It's a Perfect Education': Lifelong Learning and the Experience of Foundation-level GNVQ Students. *Journal of Vocational Education and Training,* 53 (1): 81–100.

Bell, J and Dexter, T (2002) Using Multilevel Models to Assess the Comparability of Examinations. Paper presented at *Fifth International Conference on Social Science Methodology of the Research Committee on Logic and Methodology (RC33) of the International Sociological Association* (ISA) available online at: *http://cambridgeassessment.org.uk/ca/digitalAssets/113934_Using_Multilevel_ Models_to_Assess_the_Comparability_of_Exami.pdf* accessed February 2010

Board of Education (1938) *Report of the Consultative Committee on Secondary Education with Special Reference to Grammar Schools and Technical High Schools* (Spens Report). London: HMSO.

Board of Education (1943) *Curriculum and Examinations in Secondary Schools* (Norwood Report). London: HMSO.

Brockmann, M, Clarke, L and Winch, C (2008) Knowledge, Skills, Competence: European Divergences in Vocational Education and Training (VET) – the English, German and Dutch Cases. *Oxford Review of Education*, 1465–3915, Volume 34, Issue 5, first published 2008, pages 547–567.

Brooks, R (1998) *Staying or Leaving? A Literature Review of Factors Affecting the Take-up of Post-16 Options.* Slough: NFER.

Carr, W and Hartnett, A (1996) *Education and the Struggle for Democracy.* Buckingham: Open University Press.

Clarke, J and Willis, P (1984) Introduction, in Bates, I *et al. Schooling for the Dole?: the New Vocationalism.* London: Macmillan Publishers Ltd.

Colley, H (2006) Learning to Labour with Feeling: Class, Gender and Emotion in Childcare Education and Training. *Contemporary Issues in Early Childhood,* 7 (1): 15–29.

Colley, H, James, D, Tedder, M and Diment, K (2003) Learning as Becoming in Vocational Education and Training: Class, Gender and the Role of Vocational Habitus. *Journal of Vocational Education and Training,*55 (4): 471–97.

Committee on Higher Education, *Higher Education,* Report of the Committee appointed by the Prime Minister under the Chairmanship of Lord Robbins 1961–63 (the Robbins Report), October 1963, Cmnd. 2154.

Crombie-White, R (1997) The ASDAN Award Scheme: a Celebration of Professional Practice, in Tomlinson, S (ed) *Education 14–19 Critical Perspectives.* London: The Athlone Press.

Daily Mail (2009) *Teenagers secretly taking 'O' Levels because GCSEs are 'too easy'.* 5 December 2009.

Daily Telegraph (2009) *IGCSE row as state schools are banned from offering 'rigorous' exams.* 4 December 2009.

Dearing, R (1996) *Review of Qualifications for 16–19 Year Olds Full Report*. SCAA.

Department for Children, Schools and Families/Department for Industry, Universities and Skills (2008) *Raising Expectations: Enabling the System to Deliver.* Norwich: TSO.

DES (1991) *Education and Training for the 21st Century: The Challenge to Colleges.* London: HMSO.

DfEE (1999) *Learning to Succeed: a New Framework for Post-16 Learning*. London: The Stationery Office.

DfES (2002) *14–19 Extending Opportunities, Raising Standards.* London: The Stationery Office.

DfES (2003a) *14–19 Opportunity and Excellence.* London: The Stationery Office.

DfES (2005a) *14–19 Education and Skills.* Annesley: DfES Publications.

DfES (2005b) *Realising the Potential*: *a Review of the Future Role of Further Education Colleges* (Foster Review). Annesley: DfES Publications.

DfES (2006) *Further Education: Raising Skills, Improving Life Chances.* Norwich: The Stationery Office.

Ecclestone, K (2002) *Learning Autonomy in Post-16 Education: The Politics and Practice of Formative Assessment.* London: Routledge/Falmer.

Fuller, A and Unwin, L (2003) Creating a 'Modern Apprenticeship': a Critique of the UK's Multi-sector, Social Inclusion Approach. *Journal of Education and Work,* 16 (1): 5–25.

Gleeson, D (1987) (ed) *TVEI and Secondary Education: a Critical Appraisal.* Milton Keynes: Open

University Press.

Great Britain (1895) *Royal Commission on Secondary Education (Bryce Commission) Report of the Commissioners.* London: HMSO.

Guardian (2002) *Six weeks to re-think A-Level marking* available at: *www.guardian.co.uk/education/ 2002/oct/14/alevels2002.schools*. Reproduced article originally published 14 October 2002 in *the Guardian.*

Helsby, G, Knight, P and Saunders M (1998) Preparing Students for the New Work Order: the Case of Advanced General National Vocational Qualifications. *British Educational Research Journal Volume,* 24(1): 63–78

Hodgson, A, Steer, R, Spours, K, Edward, S, Coffield, F, Finlay, I and Gregson, M (2007) Learners in the English Learning and Skills Sector: the Implications of Half-right Policy Assumptions. *Oxford Review of Education,* 33 (3): 315–30.

Hodkinson, P (1996) Careership: The Individual, Choices and Markets in the Transition to Work, in Avis, J et al. *Knowledge and Nationhood Education, Politics and Work.* London: Cassell.

Hodkinson, P, Sparkes, A and Hodkinson, H (1996) *Triumphs and Tears: Young People, Markets and the Transition from School to Work.* London: David Fulton.

The Independent (2002) *Exam crisis: 'Heads will roll' if results were manipulated.* 20 September 2002 online available at: *www.independent.co.uk/news/education/education-news/exam-crisis-heads-will-roll-if-results-were-manipulated-607412.html*

Keep, E (2004) Reflections on a Curious Absence: The Role of Employers, Labour Market Incentives and Labour Market Regulation. *Nuffield Review of 14–19 Education and Training Working Paper 22* (based on Discussion Paper given at Working Day IV, 25 May 2004) available online at: *www.nuffield14-19review.org.uk/cgi/documents/documents.cgi?a=28&t=template.htm.*

McCulloch, G (1987) History and Policy: The Politics of TVEI, in Gleeson, D (ed) *TVEI and Secondary Education: A Critical Appraisal.* Milton Keynes: Open University Press.

McCulloch, G (1994) *Educational Reconstruction: The 1944 Education Act and the Twenty First Century.* London: Woburn Press.

McCulloch, G (1995) Parity of Esteem and Tripartism, in Jenkins, E (ed) *Studies in the History of Education.* Leeds: Leeds University Press.

McCulloch, G (1998) *Failing the Ordinary Child? The Theory and Practice of Working Class Secondary Education.* Buckingham: Open University Press.

Millman, V and Weiner, G (1987) Engendering Equal Opportunities: The Case of TVEI, in Gleeson, D (ed) *TVEI and Secondary Education: A Critical Appraisal.* Milton Keynes: Open University Press.

Moore, R (1984) Schooling and the World of Work in Bates, I et al. *Schooling for the Dole?: the New Vocationalism.* Basingstoke: Macmillan Publishers Ltd.

MSC/DES (1985) *Review of Vocational Qualifications in England and Wales.* Manpower Services Commission and Department of Education and Science: HMSO.

NIACE (2009) *Annual Report 2008–2009* available online at: *www.niace.org.uk/sites/default/files/ Annual-Report-08-09.pdf*.

Pring, R (1995) *Closing The Gap: Liberal Education and Vocational Preparation.* London: Hodder and Stoughton.

Pring, R et al. (2009) *Education for All: The Future of Education and Training for 14–19 year olds.* London: Routledge.

Qualifications and Curriculum Authority (2006) *GCSEs and IGCSEs compared: GCSE and IGCSE examinations in 2005 in English, French, mathematics and science (double award).* Coventry: Qualifications and Curriculum Authority.

Raggatt, P and Williams, S (1999) *Government, Markets and Vocational Qualifications: An Anatomy of Policy.* London: Falmer Press.

Roberts, K (1993) Career Trajectories and the Mirage of Increased Social Mobility, in Bates, I and Riseborough, G (eds) *Youth and Inequality.* Buckingham: Open University Press.

> **CASE STUDY**
> **Amy, Jack and Liam**
> Amy spent ten days in a hairdressing salon as the work experience element of her Hair and Beauty Studies Diploma. As she did not have the skill to work on clients' hair, she spent her ten days sweeping the floor and making coffee for staff and clients.
>
> Jack wanted to work as an electrician and was doing a Diploma in Construction and the Built Environment. He was accepted by a national house-building company for his work placement. The company offered a highly structured programme for young people on work experience. For health and safety reasons this did not involve practical work, but consisted of observing the final stages in the building of a house and two days in the office to gain an overview of the company. As well as his time in the office, Jack spent time observing the plumbers, plasterers and decorators. He was able to spend one day observing the electrician.
>
> Liam was doing a Diploma in Retail Business. He was accepted on a work placement at a branch of a major supermarket. He was enabled, under supervision, to undertake tasks such as stacking shelves and was given the routine induction training received by all new staff. His friend, placed at a small independent store, was able to serve behind the counter, shown how to order stock and was provided with considerable insight into the running of an independent retail operation.

Discussion

These young people were all 15 at the time of their work experience, which they undertook as part of a school-based level 2 Diploma. Do you think their experience would have been different if they had been 16+? In what ways might it have been different?

Partnership delivery

The policy developments around 14–19 education recognised that each institution would not be able to offer the whole range of vocational qualifications. In the case of schools, most resources were already devoted to offering 'core' academic subjects, and the cost of setting up departments with realistic equipment and workspaces to deliver subjects such as construction or beauty therapy was prohibitive. The solution to this was to establish formal 'Partnerships', usually within an LA area, which facilitated young people to study in more than one institution. There were complexities with this however: where two or more FE colleges were involved they had been operating as competitors since 1993, when colleges were released from LA control and incorporated, resulting in a market-driven system of FE. These changes were introduced in response to the 1991 White Paper *Education and Training for the 21st Century*. Later policy documents, and changes to the funding regime, did nothing to discourage this. Additional complications arose which were related to very practical issues – if school A and school B were not on the same bus route, and young people from school A were attending sessions at school B, how would they be transported, who would bear the cost and how would the commuting time be accommodated within the school timetable? Despite these and similar issues, many partnerships evolved naturally, initially supported by the Increased Flexibility initiative.

The Increased Flexibility Programme (IFP) was formed as a result of policy described in the White Paper, *Schools: Achieving Success*, published in July 2001. It provided funding to support partnerships between FE colleges, schools and work-based learning providers, and in its early stages mostly involved young people from Key Stage 4 attending an FE local college to study for a vocational qualification. In other cases, FE teachers went into schools to deliver some vocational qualifications, which could be taught in a standard school classroom. Examples of this included Health and Social Care and Leisure and Tourism. Eventually, the expectation that partnerships would expand and develop to facilitate young people to access an ever increasing menu of vocational qualifications became a key tenet of policy in this area (see DfES, 2002; 2003). Partnerships were increasingly formalised and in the early 2000s Learning Partnerships, funded by local Learning and Skills Councils (LSCs) and working with them and with LAs, were established to promote Partnership Working across broad geographical areas. Some of these continue to function strongly and exert considerable influence on local policy, while others have much more limited scope or influence.

In 2007, The Nuffield Review of 14–19 Education advocated a move from what it termed *weakly collaborative partnerships* to the *strongly collaborative local learning systems,* which Lumby and Foskett (2005, page 133) have argued are closely associated with the vision for an integrated 14–19 phase. The policy imperative to move towards stronger systems came from a range of targets and initiatives including the introduction of a 14–19 entitlement. The paper published by the Nuffield Review proposes a model for determining the extent of collaboration in a partnership (2007, pages 4–5) but concludes that many partnerships remain *fragile*. It argues that a key reason for this is the tension that arises from being required to collaborate with organisations that are also competitors.

Difficulties associated with finance, as well as with working closely with organisations which may be in competition with one another, or have very different values, are highlighted by Lumby and Foskett (2005, Chapter 10) in their discussion around the many inherent difficulties of partnership working. In terms of finance, issues around the cost of courses, who pays and how much, have been aggravated by the different funding regimes for schools and FE colleges. The recent introduction of the Young People's Learning Agency, which brings all 14–19 funding under a single umbrella following the demise of the LSC in 2010, and the dropping of planned *in-year adjustments* to 16–19 budgets (which could have resulted in schools and colleges losing expected funding part-way through a year) may help to resolve some of these problems by providing greater financial certainty. In addition, government announcements about the future of the Diploma, and LAs' new responsibility for the strategic management of the 14–19 phase in their area are also likely to encourage the ongoing development of partnership working.

CASE STUDY

Parveen

Parveen is a childcare tutor in a large general FE college in an inner city area. She has consistently had her teaching graded at 'good' and 'outstanding'. Her approach to behaviour management has always been based on mutual respect and acknowledging that students' behaviour is often reflective of widely diverse backgrounds, experiences and cultures. She has been told by her line manager that part of her teaching during the next academic year will be the delivery of a range of childcare programmes to 14–16-year-olds from a local 11–16 school. The school has a strict and very rigid behaviour management policy, which was introduced following criticisms made during an OfSTED inspection.

Discussion

Read the case study above and then discuss the questions with your colleagues. See if, through partnership working, you can come to a consensus on the final question!

- How could Parveen reconcile her own approach to behaviour management with that of the school?
- How could the college support her in this?
- What agreement could the school and college come to which would meet the needs and values of all involved?

When you have come to a consensus on Parveen's situation, start to think about how such issues influence the provision that you are a part of, and move on to do the activity below. It may be useful to discuss this in groups, particularly if you can work with colleagues who are part of the same provision or partnership as you.

REFLECTIVE TASK

Now reflect on the organisations you work with as part of the 14–19 provision in your area. To what extent are the partnerships 'weakly' or 'strongly' collaborative? What is your evidence for this? How might collaborative activity be developed or improved?

This section has provided a brief introduction to partnership working: a more extended discussion may be found in Chapter 6.

The growth of PSHE and introduction of citizenship

Personal, Social and Health Education (sometimes personal, social, health and economic education) or PSHE and Citizenship are often taught together, although for curriculum purposes they are different subjects. Citizenship education in its current form was introduced to schools in 2002 following the publication of the Crick Report (Advisory Group on Citizenship, 1998). The Crick Report was the outcome of the deliberations of the Advisory Group on Citizenship, which was established in 1997, as part of the policy developments following the publication of the education White Paper *Excellence in Schools*. It made a number of very detailed recommendations. Key among these was that *citizenship education be a statutory entitlement in the curriculum and that all schools should be required to show they are fulfilling the obligation that this places upon them* (Advisory Group on Citizenship, 1998, page 22). Other recommendations advised on the amount of curriculum time to be devoted to the subject, the desirability of integrating citizenship with other subjects and OfSTED inspection.

The purpose of teaching citizenship as a subject in school is to equip young people to participate as active citizens in our society. A variety of initiatives and strategies to support young people to acquire practical understanding of key concepts such as democracy, justice, human rights, diversity and inequality have emerged. These include the introduction of schools councils, anti-bullying and recycling projects as well as using both citizenship and PSHE as vehicles to meet some of the requirements of the five outcomes of the Every Child Matters (ECM) agenda (see Chapter 6 for a full discussion of ECM). In addition, some schools are using short course accreditation, such as that discussed later in this chapter, to recognise citizenship learning and achievements. One example of this is the OCR Entry Level Certificate in Citizenship Studies, another is the short course GCSE in citizenship.

A longitudinal study exploring the short- and long-term effects of citizenship education was commissioned by the then Department for Education and Skills (DfES) in 2001. The study, which was conducted by NFER, ended in 2010 and reported on emerging findings annually. Its early findings indicated that levels of *individual efficacy* or the extent to which young people felt they could make a change for the better were the major influence on attitudes to civic participation. However, this personal efficacy is influenced by a range of other factors and characteristics, including age, gender and social class, meaning that there is a complex interplay of many different factors which influence civic participation (Benton *et al.*, 2008, pages 98–100).

Considering citizenship education from a philosophical perspective, Winch (2005, page 1) in his contribution to a paper co-authored with Roberts and Lambert, discusses how through civic education, young people could be *empowered to become informed, engaged, critically rational citizens of a benign, evolving liberal democracy*. Citing work by John Stuart Mill and Adam Smith, he raises concerns that a civic education might be used to indoctrinate young people with a particular political ideology, which is in conflict with notions of democracy. His solution to this problem is to ground civic education in subjects and activities which are more neutral. History is advocated as presenting the opportunity to show young people how societies develop, while civic participation – for example through voluntary activities – provides the opportunity for young people to develop *the abilities necessary to democratic politics* (*ibid*, page 4). Winch goes on to argue that although he considers contemporary vocational education to be *impoverished* and incapable of creating the conditions necessary for an effective citizenship education, a revised Diploma, which accredits activities such as voluntary work and sporting activities, could provide valuable opportunities for engagement with civil society in the way he advocates.

REFLECTIVE TASK

Explore the following questions in writing, and use them to consider the idea of citizenship education. If you want to explore this in more depth, you could read the paper on citizenship education that is cited above to inform your ideas. The paper is available online at www.nuffield14-19review.org.uk/.

- What are the three key values and principles you hold?
- What were the influences, experiences and activities that led to those principles and values?
- What contribution do you make to wider society?
- What were the influences, experiences and activities that led to you making that contribution?
- How were these related to your educational experiences?
- What sort of citizenship education do you believe could best enable young people to develop their own values and support them to contribute to society?

PSHE, while often taught together with citizenship, is, in fact, a different subject or set of subjects. Although PSHE is offered by most schools, it is not mandatory, although some aspects of it – such as sex and relationship education – are. It is currently taught through two interrelated programmes in secondary schools, one of which is focused on personal and social issues and one on financial and economic education. It is not a subject that is taught in colleges, although some aspects of the college curriculum cover similar material: these vary from college to college, and, to an extent, depend on the approach the individual institution has taken to meeting the ECM outcomes. For example, some college tutorial programmes now cover aspects of health education.

A major review into PSHE – which encompasses drugs and alcohol education; emotional health and well-being; sex and relationship education; nutrition and physical activity; personal finance; safety; careers education and work-related learning – was conducted by Sir Alasdair Macdonald in 2009. The review was commissioned due to government concerns over the variability of PSHE education and the perceived need to *support children and young people's personal development and wellbeing* (Macdonald, 2009, page 12). While promoted by government policy, and regarded as positive and helpful by many practitioners, many of the approaches used in PSHE have also been subject to vocal criticism. Strategies such as peer mentoring and personalisation in secondary schools have been argued to be a development of activities such as Social and Emotional Aspects of Learning (SEAL) and circle time in primary schools, and the use of subjects such as drama, English, biology and history to promote contested concepts such as emotional literacy have been criticised as diluting the curriculum and *turning humanistic and holistic education into humanitarian education* (Ecclestone and Hayes, 2009, pages 59–64). Arguments such as those made by Ecclestone and Hayes suggest that the integration of activities related to personal growth and emotional development across the curriculum assume that all young people have difficulties in these areas, thus pathologising them, and create a curriculum which is more focused on emotional issues than subject teaching, resulting in an impoverished education which ultimately disadvantages young people, and leads to a diminished self (Ecclestone, 2007; Ecclestone and Hayes 2009).

Similar arguments have been made about the curriculum and many of the support services and mechanisms in FE which have proliferated in recent years. Examples of such services would be counselling, anger management groups and on-site health drop-in centres; also part of this ethos around support and therapy are some aspects of the curriculum and forms of assessment. It is easy to take the growth of an area of the curriculum, such as PSHE, for granted and to believe that it has always been there and there has always been a need to support young people in particular areas. However, this is not the case. As reflected in Chapter 2, the concerns around vocational education 30 years ago related to the curriculum and the way it was, or was not, preparing young people for employment. Issues around behaviour, or the need for support, were not discussed; this has been a relatively recent development in literature and government policy. Reflecting this, as recently as 1995 Rees wrote about a *growing tide* (of young people with emotional and behavioural difficulties) and argued that the FE sector *urgently needs to address strategies, systems and policies to deal with students who have emotional and behavioural difficulties* (Rees, 1995, page 97).

Rees' argument suggests that these were then relatively new issues in the sector. Since then, many different strategies and systems have been put in place to support learners with such difficulties and this has included curricular developments such as the growth of PSHE in schools, mirrored by similar activities which are integrated into tutorial sessions or the curriculum in colleges. It is useful to reflect on these changes over time and think about their impact on institutions, individuals and the curriculum.

Think about the following two questions and record your answers.

- To what extent are PSHE issues embedded in the subject you teach/the curriculum your students follow?
- What are the benefits and disadvantages of this? (Try to come up with at least three of each.)

Do the benefits outweigh the disadvantages or the advantages outweigh the disadvantages? Discuss the reasons for your view with colleagues.

Short course accreditation

Many of the activities suggested by Winch (see above, page 37) as a means of promoting citizenship education are already available to many young people as alternative forms of education, which are accredited as 'short courses'. The ASDAN awards are particularly good examples of this.

ASDAN is a charity which also operates as an Awarding Body, and which has, for many years, offered a wide range of short courses broadly related to Personal and Social Development which can be achieved by contributing to wider society. These can be taken individually, or as part of the nationally recognised Certificate of Personal Effectiveness, which is accredited at levels 1 and 2. The 12 modules cover a range of activities including Communication, Citizenship and Community, Sport and Leisure and Independent Living. Aimed at the 14–19 population, the success of the Certificate is reflected in the number of annual registrations for the award – 150,000 in any one year (Pring *et al.,* 2009, page 80). Other examples of short course accreditation are those provided by the Awarding Body Open College Network (OCN). Like ASDAN, the OCN is a charity and, similarly to ASDAN, is committed to relieving disadvantage through widening participation and providing inclusive learning opportunities. OCN offers Awards, Certificates and Diplomas within the new framework from Entry level to level 3.

This type of short course accreditation is used by some schools and colleges to recognise learning in specific areas of the curriculum, such as in citizenship (see above), drama or outdoor learning activities. Awards such as those offered through ASDAN and OCN are also used, mainly in FE colleges and on Entry to Employment (E2E) provision, to provide personalised 'pic'n'mix' programmes of learning. These tend to be widening participation programmes which are designed for marginalised learners such as young people who have learning difficulties, those who are disaffected or disengaged with education and those who are or have been NEET (Not in Employment, Education or Training). The value of these programmes is that they allow each individual to collect small accreditations, which can be included on a CV or Record of Achievement. Such programmes seek to re-engage young people and facilitate them to progress to more mainstream provision and eventually into employment. Such accreditation is also offered by significant numbers of community-based, charitable organisations that work with socially excluded groups. An example of this type of provision is given below.

disapproval. Consequently, the government was not prepared to accept the recommendations of the Working Group on 14–19 Reform, and instead, against the advice of Tomlinson, chose *further piecemeal changes* (ibid). The final position adopted by the government was to implement a modified version of the recommendations, focusing principally on the introduction of new vocational Diplomas and, over time, introducing a number of more academically based Diplomas. The schedule for introduction of the new Diplomas is shown below.

	Date of introduction			
	September 2008	September 2009	September 2010	September 2011
Line of learning	• Construction and the Built Environment • Information Technology • Engineering • Creative and Media • Society, Health and Development	• Environmental and Land-based Studies • Manufacturing and Product Design • Hair and Beauty Studies • Hospitality • Business Administration and Finance	• Public Services • Sport and Active Leisure • Retail Business • Travel and Tourism	• Humanities • Languages • Science

Table 4.1: Timetable for the introduction of 14–19 Diplomas (source: DCSF, 2009, page 10).

REFLECTIVE TASK

The government has stated that *by 2013, every young person, will be entitled to take the diploma of their choice, in their local area* (DCSF, 2009, page 8). Which of the 17 Diplomas are already available or will be available in your organisation? Where will learners be able to study the other Diplomas that will not be delivered in your workplace? What are the local arrangements for the delivery of all 17 lines of learning in your area, to support the government in achieving its aim?

Tomlinson's original aim that *all* young people would engage in learning under a single unified framework was not accepted and, instead, five discrete pathways for young people, including the Diploma, were identified. These pathways are shown in the central column of Table 4.2 below. Rather than being a unified approach, the Diploma now represented just one of the options available to young people. However, once young people had embarked on a route, this would not mean that they had to remain locked into that learning pathway for all time, and they would *be able to choose or change paths at the end of key stage 3, and at 16, 17 and 18* (ibid, page 3). The approach adopted by the government is illustrated in Table 4.2 below.

Options available to 14-year-olds (end of Key Stage 3/Year 10)	Options available to 16- and 17-year-olds (end of Key Stage 4/Year 12)	Options available to 18-year-olds (post compulsory schooling)
• GCSEs • Foundation or Higher Diploma • Foundation Learning Tier	• GCSEs/A levels • Higher Diploma or Advanced Diploma • Foundation Learning Tier • Apprenticeship • Employment with training	• Higher education • Further education • Employment • Apprenticeship • Employment with training

Table 4.2: Learning pathways available from 2008 (source: DCSF, 2009, page 34).

REFLECTIVE TASK

Although all pathways need to be available to a young person, it is not expected that every institution will provide each pathway. What are the arrangements in your organisation for accessing Foundation, Higher and Advanced Diplomas? What guidance is given to young people who wish to enter employment or to follow an apprenticeship? How are young people supported to access further and higher education? What difference has this new framework made to existing practices in your workplace?

One of the principal motivations for developing the Diploma pathway was a recognition that *too many young people leave education lacking basic and personal skills* (Working Group on 14–19 Reform, 2004, page 1). The Diplomas were designed to provide every young person with the opportunity to develop *the generic knowledge, skills and attributes necessary for participation in higher education, working life and the community* (*ibid*, page 5). While not accepting the recommendations of the Tomlinson Report in full, the development of key and basic skills remained a stated aim of the government's response to Tomlinson and it declared it would *ensure that every young person has a sound grounding in the basics of English and maths and the skills they need for employment* (DfES, 2005a, page 4) and that *irrespective of the path a young person chooses, every student will be taught functional skills in maths, English and ICT* (DCSF, 2009, page). Further, the government committed to the idea that *personal, learning and thinking (PLT) skills are also built into all routes* (*ibid*), and those students who elected to follow the Diploma pathway, would be guaranteed the *equivalent of a day each week learning practical skills relevant to the sector covered by the Diploma and delivered by people with real industry experience in high quality, professional surroundings* (DfES, 2005b, page 14).

To a degree then, the government was prepared to accept some of Tomlinson's proposals and to try and implement practices that would:

• help to increase the basic skills level of young people;
• equip them with the understanding needed to enter employment;
• remove some of the confusion in relation to the qualifications framework.

However, rather than take the bold, progressive approach advocated by Tomlinson, it appears the government elected to make modifications to the existing system and add to the current range of qualifications to achieve these aims – whether or not such an approach will be successful remains to be seen.

Teaching methods for younger learners

The changes that the government was prepared to adopt signalled a *managed evolution* (Working Group on 14–19 Reform, 2004, page 1) of the education system. This new approach to learning necessarily required a new approach to teaching. However, being able to effectively teach is directly influenced by students' readiness to learn. Moreover, *how do you motivate the unmotivated* (Wallace, 2007, page xi) or cope with *unruly learners who are bored, restless, fed up, noisy and keen to do anything but engage in any kind of learning activity?* (ibid).

While accepting that not all young people are the same or learn in the same way, almost as an inevitable feature of their age, younger learners are more likely to:

- lack a clear sense of purpose when learning;
- not have developed the skills they need to be independent learners;
- be unable to concentrate for long periods of time;
- not understand how to structure or use their time productively;
- lack maturity;
- take longer to settle to a given task;
- be resistant to engaging in more passive activities, such as reading.

Your responsibility as a tutor is not only to teach the principal subject the learners are studying, but to also to find approaches that will successfully engage them and help them to develop effective learning habits which they will be able to use in your session and in other learning environments.

Strategies to engage younger learners

When working with younger learners you may need to modify or change your usual approach to teaching. The following strategies are useful ways to encourage younger learners to participate in learning.

- *Break your session into 'bite-sized' learning sections* –If learners are presented with large sections of what appear to be dense and complicated ideas, or simply too much information, it is possible they may switch off before even attempting tasks. Although you may have a clear understanding of your scheme of work and how different learning activities relate to each other, this may be very difficult for your learners to understand. Sometimes, learners need to have their learning broken down into small, easy to understand sections, which build up into a bigger picture. This may mean that instead of asking a learner to create a play-zone for children as part of a construction project, you would direct them to complete relevant background research, help them to identify suitable materials, assist them in drawing up appropriate plans and support them in making scale models of their design before they were required to embark in a large-scale project. Effectively, you are providing a framework that allows learners to complete work in multiple mini-stages.
- *Provide active learning opportunities* – Some younger learners find it difficult to engage with passive learning methods such as listening to a lecture or watching a programme. For these students you need to find ways to include more learning activity. Rather than asking your creative and media students to critique an advert for a new clothes shop, ask them to produce a script, act in it and film their own advert. Using an active learning approach that encourages learner participation helps students to remember the work covered. This is illustrated in the learning pyramid below.

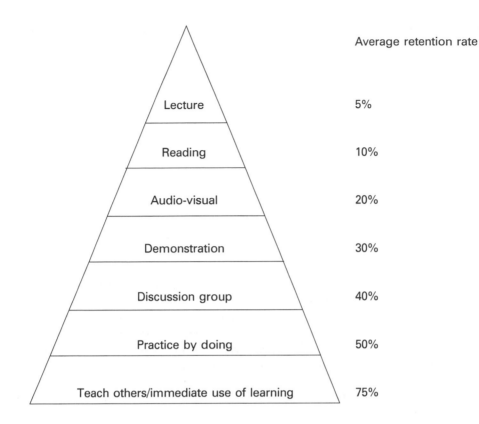

Average retention rate

Lecture	5%
Reading	10%
Audio-visual	20%
Demonstration	30%
Discussion group	40%
Practice by doing	50%
Teach others/immediate use of learning	75%

Figure 4.1: The learning pyramid (information based on research undertaken by the National Training Laboratories, Bethel, in Maine, USA).

- *Give clear instructions* – Use precise, unambiguous language when working with younger learners. Avoid phrases such as 'you may like to...' if you are not offering the learners a real choice. Instead, use direct language and tell the learners what they need to do to complete a task. Give instructions in the order in which you would like the instructions completed. Choice can often be confusing for students, and they may struggle with the concept of equally valid alternatives. Try to keep your instructions to a minimum. While most younger learners should be able to recall a short list of three or four items, they may find it difficult to remember a longer or more complex set of instructions. In this situation, support your learners by giving them as many cues as possible to help them to remember. You may find it helpful to tell the learners what they need to do, show them how they should complete the task and provide them with a task sheet that lists your instructions. It may also be helpful to display these instructions somewhere in the room. Learners with limited literacy skills may benefit from having instructions presented in a diagrammatic or graphic format.
- *Provide learners with templates to record their learning* – Sometimes learners are able to complete the learning activities you have planned, but struggle to record their work and lack the skills to identify how they should present their work. This can be a real problem and learners may feel demotivated that having completed the necessary work, they cannot complete the final hurdle. You can support learners here by giving them a pre-formatted template to record their work on. This may be as simple as giving learners the key headings they would need to use to record their work; it might be providing them with a set of task sheets with guidance describing what they need to do to complete each section; or it could be a

on the college site to both school and college students because the college had better accommodation and resources; and the college and school shared delivery of the information technology Diploma, providing another opportunity for students from both organisations to mix with each other. All students studying the Diploma route, whether at college or school, were able to take part in work experience and project activities.

REFLECTIVE TASK

Streamside College and Glenmore Grange School represent one model for delivering the Diploma. What features would you identify as good practice? In what ways do you feel that this working arrangement could be improved? What benefits can you identify for the college, the school and local businesses in working in this way? Would you assess this to be a partnership of equals or do you feel that some organisations appear to be deriving more benefit than others? What future developments do you perceive are necessary? In comparison to Streamside College and Glenmore Grange School, how well do you believe your organisation is performing in delivering the Diploma?

Planning to deliver the Diploma

The diploma is a new 14–19 qualification that brings an innovative approach to learning. It enables learners to gain knowledge, understanding and hands-on experience of sectors they are interested in, while putting new skills into practice.

Created to provide a real alternative to more traditional education and qualifications, diplomas represent the most important change to the country's education system since the introduction of GCSEs. Diplomas are a fully rounded qualification combining theoretical with practical learning – including functional English, mathematics and information technology (ICT). The aim is to equip young people with the skills, knowledge and understanding they will need for further or higher education, as well as for their long-term employability.

(QIA, 2008, page 2)

All Diplomas are organised into three main learning areas.

1. Principal learning – this enables learners to develop the knowledge, understanding, skills and attitudes that supports progress in the chosen line of learning into the specific subject or employment area concerned.

2. Generic learning – this supports learners to develop the transferable skills they will need for today's world. Generic learning comprises functional skills (English, numeracy/mathematics and ICT); personal, learning and thinking skills; foundation, higher or extended project; and work experience.

3. Additional and specialist learning – this provides breadth and/or depth to the learning experience without duplication of learning elsewhere.

The guided learning hours (GLH) for each learning area, together with an indication of total taught hours, according to Diploma level is shown in Table 4.3 below.

Diploma level	Principal learning component	Generic learning component	Additional and specialist learning component
Foundation total GLH = 600	240 GLH	Functional skills: 120 GLH Foundation project: 60 GLH Personal, learning and thinking skills: 60 GLH Work experience = 10 days minimum	120 GLH
Higher total GLH = 800	420 GLH	Functional skills = 80 GLH Higher project = 60 GLH Personal, learning and thinking skills = 60 GLH Work experience = 10 days minimum	180 GLH
Advanced total GLH = 1080	540 GLH	Extended project = 120 GLH Personal, learning and thinking skills = 60 GLH Work experience = 10 days minimum	360 GLH

Table 4.3: Guided learning hours (GLH) allocated by Diploma level and component (adapted from QIA, 2008, pages 13–14).

Within the principal learning component, learning is organised into a series of units. For the Foundation and Higher Diplomas, units are either 30 or 60 GLH, and for the Advanced Diploma units may be 30, 60 or 90 GLH.

One of the key challenges facing Diploma providers is how to organise the curriculum so that all areas of learning are effectively covered and that best use is made of available human and physical resources. Because *no single institution is likely to have all the facilities to deliver the diploma effectively... institutions are expected to collaborate in two ways: in 14–19 partnerships and in consortia* (QIA, 2008, page 94). Well-organised partnership and consortia arrangements are key to the successful delivery of the Diploma.

Different regions will generate different solutions to the operational concerns they face, and there is no model template that colleges and schools are being directed to adopt. Rather, it is expected that organisations will generate custom-made solutions to local issues. While it is not possible to identify all of the concerns that organisations will face, some of the common operational issues that many organisations will need to consider are discussed in greater detail in Chapter 6.

Assessing the Diploma

Assessment is a principal feature of any learning programme. It is *not a bolt-on extra to teaching and training but an integral part of planning preparation and delivery* (Cotton, 2002, page 5) and needs to be considered from the very outset. For the Diploma, assessment achieves two main functions.

- *It provides a means of enabling learners to achieve a national qualification. This fits in with 'assessment of learning' strategies;*

> • *It helps identify learners' ongoing progress against their own aims and targets as they move through the diploma. This fits in with 'assessment of learning' strategies.*
>
> (QIA, 2008, page 55)

It is likely that you are already using a variety of formative and summative assessment strategies, and many of these will be suitable to use for the Diploma. However, a critical feature of both of these types of assessment is they *must* be useful to the learner and help them to progress and achieve. You can support learners in achieving by developing systems that allow you to recognise and record learners' full range of achievement across a variety of different learning situations, rather than constraining them to a narrow band of assessment opportunities.

To further support learners in progressing you will need to ensure that you provide high quality feedback to learners that identifies their strengths and also highlights further areas for improvement. To achieve this you will need to make certain that your feedback is:

- timely – ideally your feedback needs to be given as close to task completion as is practically possible. In this way it is more likely that learners will be able to remember what they have done and will more readily understand what you are saying to them;
- expressed in terms that learners can understand – sometimes, teachers and tutors develop a coded way of speaking that is understood by other teachers and tutors, but which is not clear to learners. Without being brutal, which may have a negative impact on learners, find ways to write and say what you need to in terms that are accessible to learners;
- measured – you may feel that learners need to improve in at least 14 different ways. Although this may be true, it is unlikely that learners will be able to accommodate such a quantity of feedback. Instead, choose to focus on the principal points where improvement is of most importance. That way, it is likely that learners will be able to both understand what is required of them and will be able to act on any advice they receive;
- realistic – while it is important to have high expectations of, and aspirations for, learners, it is also important to recognise levels of achievement. Set learners challenging, but not impossible, goals in your feedback and offer support to help them attain these goals;
- focused – offer feedback that concentrates on the most significant issues raised by the work. As far as you are able to, in both written and verbal feedback, remember to use the 'feedback sandwich' technique and balance points for improvement with positive messages. Always leave the learner in a position where they are motivated to want to make improvements to their work and are inspired to do so. Try not to leave learners demoralised and feeling they would like to leave the course;
- collaborative – wherever and whenever you can seek to engage the learners in assessment. This may be asking learners to evaluate their own performance or could be involving their peers in the assessment of their work. Assessment needs to consider both the outcomes of learning, the product, and also the way in which students engaged with learning, *the process*. Students will be aware of many features and facets which will be difficult for you to collect evidence of. This could include manual skills such as demonstrating competence in practical tasks like measuring, or evidencing verbal skills, for example, responding appropriately to a customer complaint. Try to use learners as critical friends, who are in the position to assist you, and their peers, in the development of learning.

Once you have assessed learners you will need to log the evidence of their achievements. This is so that you can confirm that learners have achieved the standards required at different levels.

PRACTICAL TASK PRACTICAL TASK **PRACTICAL TASK** PRACTICAL TASK **PRACTICAL TASK**

From Table 4.4 below, focus on one or two of the characteristics and identify strategies that you could try out in a series of lessons.

Characteristics	Examples of teaching strategies in lesson	Impact on learning
Help learners to recognise the standards they are aiming for	You could: • explain criteria for success • model success by providing examples	Learners will be able to: • understand the standards expected of them • recognise the features of good work
Involve learners in peer and self- assessment	You could: • help learners to interpret learning outcomes • provide opportunities for learners to discuss their work • allow time for learners to reflect on their learning	Learners will be able to: • assess the progress they have made • identify how they can improve their work • act as critical friends
Provide feedback that supports learners in recognising the next steps they need to take	You could: • question learners in groups about their work • give oral feedback • use examples of work in class to show how improvements can be achieved	Learners will be able to: • discuss developments with peers (PLTS) • learn from each other
Promote confidence so that every learner can improve	You could: • provide positive and constructive feedback • set targets and challenges • celebrate success	Learners will be able to: • remain engaged and on task • gain satisfaction in their work • develop a sense that they can continually improve

Table 4.4: Assessment for learning–key characteristics (adapted from QIA, 2008, pages 64–5).

Once learners have completed the programme, they will be awarded a Diploma, providing they have achieved *all components within the diploma, including PLTS, functional skills and additional and specialist learning and the project* (ibid, page 80). The grading structure for Foundation, Higher and Advanced Diplomas is shown in Table 4.5 below.

Diploma level	Grades available
Foundation	A*, A, B, or ungraded, U
Higher	A*, A, B, C or ungraded, U
Advanced	A*, A, B, C,D, E or ungraded, U

Table 4.5 Grading structure for the Diploma by level (adapted from QIA, 2008, page 80).

A SUMMARY OF **KEY POINTS**

The Diploma is a new qualification. Although many colleges and schools have experience of delivering vocational programmes, the way that the Diploma is organised and the range of learning components that make up the Diploma make it distinctly different from other vocational qualifications. This has brought with it a range of new challenges for organisations to manage and a variety of potential opportunities for organisations to explore.

This chapter has explored:

> the contextual background of the Diploma;

> the range of Diplomas available and their timetable for introduction;

> the different study pathways open to young people at 14, 16 and 18;

> teaching strategies suited to younger learners within the context of the Diploma;

> different teaching settings for the delivery of the Diploma;

> the structure of the Diploma;

> issues in assessing the Diploma.

REFERENCES REFERENCES REFERENCES **REFERENCES** REFERENCES REFERENCES

Cotton, J (2002) *The Theory of Assessment.* London: Kogan Page.

DCSF (2009) *14–19 Briefing: Making Change Happen.* London: HMSO.

DfES (2005a) *14–19 Education and Skills.* London: HMSO Available online at *www.dfes.gov.uk/ publications/14-19educationandskills*

DfES(2005b) *14–19 Education and Skills – Implementation Plan.* Annesley: DfES Publications.

The Learning Pyramid. Available online at *www.teachinontario.ca/.../En/3b_strategies.html*

Quality Improvement Agency (2008) *Practitioner Guide to the Diploma – Delivering the 14–19 Education and Skills Programme.* London: Ashford Colour Press. Available online at *www.diploma-support.org/system/files/diploma-guide-prelims.pdf*

Wallace, S (2007) *Getting the Buggers Motivated in FE.* London: Continuum.

Working Group on 14–19 Reform (2004) *14–19 Curriculum and Qualifications Reform – Final Report of the Working Group on 14–19 Reform.* Annesley: DfES Publications.

FURTHER READING FURTHER READING **FURTHER READING** FURTHER READING

DCSF (2009) *14–19 Reform, Nuts and Bolts series – Implementation Planning.* London: HMSO. Available online at: *www.dcsf.gov.uk/14-19/document/implementation_planning_nuts_bolts.pdf*

Hodgson, A and Spours, K (2008) *Education and Training 14–19, Curriculum, Qualifications and Organisation.* London: Sage.

Petty, G (2004) *Teaching Today.* Cheltenham: Nelson Thornes.

Pring, R *et al.* (2009) *Education For All – the Future of Education and Training for 14–19 year olds.* Abingdon: Routledge.

QCA (2008) *The Diploma and its Pedagogy.* Available online at *www.qca.gov.uk/libraryAssets/media/ The_Diploma_and_its_pedagogy.pdf*

Race, P and Pickford, R (2008) *Making Teaching Work – Teaching Smarter in Post-compulsory Education.* London: Sage.

Wallace, S (2007) *Teaching, Tutoring and Training in the Lifelong Learning Sector (3rd ed).* Exeter: Learning Matters.

Websites

www.teachingideas.co.uk/more/management/contents.htm
http://www.diploma-support.org/
www.ofqual.gov.uk
http://teachingandlearning.qia.org.uk/tlp/pedagogy/introducingthe1/index.html

5
Managing the behaviour of 14–19-year-olds in colleges

The objectives of this chapter

This chapter will explore strategies that can be used to help to create a positive working atmosphere and ways to support learners in college. It will consider issues in managing the behaviour of younger learners within a college environment along with some of the challenges (and potential opportunities) presented in working with this age group. It will examine the responsibilities of working with 14–16-year-olds and review potential behaviour management strategies that may be useful in this context.

This chapter provides support in helping you to achieve the following Professional Standards needed to gain QTLS status:

- **Understand how to create an environment which supports learning (AK4.1; BK1.1; BK 1.2; BK1.3; BP1.3).**
- **Reflect on your own personal practice and the choices you make when teaching (AK4.2; BK2.6).**
- **Identify a range of behaviour management strategies that may be useful to you in your work (BK1.2).**
- **Understand some of the issues which relate to working with 14–16-year-old learners in colleges (AK6.1; AK6.2).**
- **Consider communication strategies that promote effective dialogue with this age range (BP3.1; BP3.2; BP3.4).**

The evolution of college learning communities – a brief history

Before considering the issues involved with managing younger learners in colleges, it is worthwhile to take time to remember how college learning communities have evolved over time, and how FE came to provide for such a diverse clientele. FE has its own unique character and is distinctly different from other education providers such as secondary schools or training organisations. To a certain extent, this difference arises because of its historical development and the way that FE colleges came into existence. And, to a degree, it is this unique character that has influenced the type of learners who choose or may even be encouraged to study in colleges.

Most further education colleges have grown from either the former mechanics' institutes or technical schools (Hall, 1994, page 2). Mechanics' Institutes were independent organisations established in the 1800s to provide technical education to working adult males and to promote appropriate social attitudes among the working population. These Institutes were welcomed by the new, emergent class of skilled industrial workers and artisans, who viewed them as providing an opportunity to help improve their knowledge base. It was not until nearly the start of the twentieth century that the government assumed a co-ordinating role in the development of technical skills by providing funding to create *a range of technical colleges* (Lucas, 2004, page 9), which, as part of the 1944 Education Act, were later replaced by technical secondary schools and county technical colleges. Like the Mechanics' Institutes before them, both the technical secondary schools and technical colleges were designed to meet the needs of industry and to facilitate entry to work for young people. It was these technical colleges through a series of further Acts and interventions (for example, the 1956 White Paper on Technical Education, the 1961 White Paper on Training Opportunities, the 1964 Industrial Training Act and the 1992 Further and Higher Education Act) that evolved into the FE colleges we know today.

The 1944 Education Act determined that the primary function of FE was to provide *full-time and part-time education for persons over compulsory school age* (Frankel and Reeves, 1996, page 7). It is important to remember that in 1944 pupils could leave schools at 14 and it is therefore possible younger learners may have chosen to continue their studies in colleges. However, the potential inclusion of 14-year-olds in colleges at this time was coincidental rather than strategically planned, and the critical determinant for studying at college was that learners needed to be over school leaving age. As the school leaving age was increased, these younger learners were excluded from the college population.

From the 1970s onwards colleges started to consider the needs of a broader range of learners and *Colleges increasingly saw themselves as 'responsive' institutions that not only served the needs of local employers but also the needs of individuals in the wider community, catering for a more diverse student population* (Lucas, 2004, page 19). During the 1980s colleges attempted to *cater for everyone* (Green and Lucas, 2000, page 35) and became characterised by their ever-increasing diversity. Since the 1990s FE colleges have been encouraged to expand even further and have become a key part of successive government strategies for *achieving higher levels of skills and qualifications* (Lucas, 2004, page 29) across the nation. Part of this expansion has been the introduction of the Increased Flexibility Programme (IFP).

The IFP was introduced into schools and colleges in 2002 to provide *vocational learning for 14 to 16 year olds* (Ofsted, 2005, page 1) who would benefit from being in a different learning environment. To achieve this aim, secondary schools entered into partnerships with FE colleges who were able to provide the *more diverse curriculum* (ibid, page 2) identified as appropriate for some young people. Under this provision, young people were able to attend FE colleges for part of the week to study *National Vocational Qualifications (NVQs) or other vocational qualifications* (ibid, page 2) while still enrolled at school. These have included such courses as hair and beauty, motor vehicle maintenance and construction. The IFP has been so successful that it has expanded each year since its introduction and many more young people are now studying for qualifications at FE colleges.

The client group attending FE colleges has therefore evolved over time and while FE continues to be influenced by the needs of industry and meeting the needs of employers, its client group has significantly changed during its history. Although the early Mechanics' Institutes were solely attended by adult males interested in gaining skills useful for work, modern FE colleges service the needs of a far more diverse population and, through initiatives such as the IFP, younger learners are now able to participate in college courses.

PRACTICAL TASK PRACTICAL TASK **PRACTICAL TASK** PRACTICAL TASK **PRACTICAL TASK**

It is likely that the college where you work has experienced significant changes in the groups of learners who attend the college. Try to map these changes for the last ten years. Try to specifically identify when your college started to provide programmes for school students. Over this time, what sort of groups have you noticed coming into college?

REFLECTIVE TASK

What is the prevailing attitude among the teaching staff to these changes? What has been the impact of having younger learners around? What do you believe the general response is to having school-aged students on the premises? What benefits can you identify to having these learners at college? Are there any difficulties created by having younger learners attend?

Establishing a framework for learning

Some of you may have watched the television series *The Unteachables* in which Phil Beadle worked closely with a group of disaffected school students to persuade them of the merits of learning. Others of you may be familiar with Jamie Oliver's series *Jamie's Kitchen* in which he guided post-16 students through their first catering exams. In both of these series there was a significant resource input, in terms of staffing levels and materials, together with the added attraction of being on the television. And yet, even in these extremely supportive environments, some learners presented such significant challenges that they failed, were excluded from, or chose to drop out of the programme. However, it is important to remember that given a suitable framework most students will choose to learn for most of the time and very few students are *so purposefully malevolent as to set out on a planned campaign of disruption* (Smith and Laslett, 2002, page 12).

In many ways, while not undermining the considerable benefit that many learners gained from being involved in these projects, they represented somewhat unusual, if not artificial, learning environments. You will be very fortunate indeed if you are able to secure such a generous resource allocation for your own teaching environments. However, it is very likely you will be faced with some, if not all, of the challenges identified in these two series. How will you work with the ill-prepared, late, poorly organised, sullen, aggressive or abusive learner? What will you do to persuade the argumentative, hostile or passive resistor to engage? How will you redirect the restless, unsettled, unfocused or hyperactive student to calm down and concentrate on their studies?

Your role, as manager and facilitator of learning, is to work within your environment to establish a climate which promotes learning and which enables learners to succeed.

Teaching to motivate

Motivating learners so they want to learn is central to creating a positive learning environment and, in many ways, is the most significant challenge tutors face. Your task is to demonstrate to the different client groups you teach that learning can be a beneficial, helpful and even an enjoyable experience which learners will be able to use and apply both in and beyond the classroom. Your challenge is to make this apparent to your learners. However, motivating learners is a complex issue because learners themselves are complex and different. There are no universal solutions that, once applied, will guarantee success for each and every learner. However, the following strategies, when applied consistently, will help to motivate students and enable you to more effectively manage your sessions.

- *Have as few rules as possible* – The fewer rules you have the more likely it is they will be followed and remembered. Ideally, you should aim to generate these rules in collaboration with the learners you teach. This increases their sense of ownership and makes it more likely that rules will be adhered to. Ensure that whatever rules exist they are consistently applied. Whereas sanctions may be an important part of codes of conduct for secondary schools, these should be used sparingly in an FE context, as they may remind learners of more punitive approaches. Your aim is to support learners to move to a position where they take responsibility for their own actions and accept that in an adult environment certain forms of behaviour are expected. If, however, it becomes necessary to apply sanctions *use the least intrusive* (Hook and Vass, 2007, page 123) punishments that you can.
- *Learn names of all the learners* – Within college environments it is usual to address staff by their first names. It is a politeness to ensure that you actually know the names of all your learners and it is a courtesy to pronounce their names correctly, in the same way you would expect learners to use your name correctly. The use of first names between staff and students is a small, but very significant difference between schools and colleges. It is an open reminder that hierarchies are, to a degree, flattened out within colleges and that all college users have an entitlement to be treated with equal respect. Most learners notice this difference and virtually all learners appreciate it.
- *Arrive at your sessions on time* – Punctuality is expected of learners and you should model this behaviour by arriving to the session on time. Arriving late to sessions creates the impression that the learners are not worth arriving on time for. Arriving late also provides an opportunity for some learners to engage in *idling, chatter and other unproductive activities* (Smith and Laslett, 2002, page 3), which will then need to be calmed down. By arriving on time you can meet and greet the class, swiftly establish the tone of the session and ensure order prevails from the very outset. It is an opportunity to reaffirm positive relationships and spend a few moments exchanging civil courtesies with your learners.
- *Clearly set out the aims of the session* – It is easier for learners to achieve your expectations, (and learning goals) if it is clear what you actually want them to do. This may not occur right at the very beginning of the lesson, as you may have a routine of some sort of starter or settling-in activity, but it needs to be in the beginning section of the lesson and ideally within the first ten minutes. If you are concerned that this may 'give away the answer' and remove the discovery aspect of your lesson, frame your objectives using exploratory language, for example, 'we will investigate', 'we are going to consider the relationship between' or 'we will review'. Include yourself in these aims by using 'we', to emphasise the joint nature of learning activities
- *Be as mobile as possible when teaching* – Consider the entire classroom, laboratory or workshop as the learning space and *move* between all areas. In this way you reinforce the idea that you want to work with the whole group, and you send a clear message that you are manager of the entire working space. By coming out from behind your tutor table and mingling with the learners you are sending a positive message about classroom hierarchies and it becomes easier for you to offer help to anyone who needs it. This approach also allows you unobtrusively to monitor learner progress. 'No-go' zones should not exist and it is your professional responsibility to support all learners, even the most challenging students who purposely congregate towards the back of the room in the hope they will escape your attention.
- *In the first instance ask learners to follow instructions* – Consistent with the approach that learners are now in an adult learning environment and deserve the respect you would accord to other adults, ask, rather than direct students to carry out your instructions. There is a significant qualitative difference between 'I'd like you to turn to page 43' and 'Turn to page 43'. One is a request indicating you believe that as responsible adult learners, students are likely to comply with reasonable requests, politely made, while the other signals you believe that learners are still children only able to follow direct commands. Within any learning environment there may be occasions when you simply forget to ask and appear to

You can start to build relationships with your learners by establishing a positive rapport. To do this you will need to demonstrate respect for your learners. You can show that you respect learners by:

- actively listening to them when they speak to you;
- giving them time to talk and not butting in;
- showing you value what they have to say;
- finding opportunities to spend time with learners outside of the class;
- avoiding unnecessary confrontations;
- ensuring learners are enabled to retain a sense of dignity;
- engineering win/win situations;
- taking time to explain information in understandable language.

Once you have established an atmosphere of mutual respect and reciprocal trust not only will your learners be more motivated to participate in your sessions, but you will find teaching much more rewarding.

REFLECTIVE TASK

How well do you really feel you know the groups that you teach? Do you know anything about their family life? Whether or not they have any siblings, what level of responsibility they have within their family unit? Do they need to make a financial contribution to the home? Are they are estranged or choose to live away from their original family and home? How do they feel about learning? What supports or hinders their learning? Who are their friends? What are their interests?

Supporting learners to participate

Some learners, over the course of their educational careers, have learnt not to participate. For these learners, disengagement has become their default position and they give the impression of actively choosing not to learn. It will have taken months, possibly years, for this level of disenchantment to build up. The reasons for this type of disillusionment are likely to be complex and complicated but may include:

- a lack of understanding of the subject;
- hesitancy or reluctance to engage;
- active resistance to learning;
- hate.

These attitudes to learning can be represented on a continuum, and as each position represents a different level of antipathy, each will require a different strategy.

lack of understanding $\longrightarrow$ reluctance $\longrightarrow$ active resistance to learning $\longrightarrow$ hate

increasing levels of resistance towards learning

Figure 5.1: Attitudes towards learning.

Working with learners' lack of understanding

This presents the lowest level of resistance. It is like standing on the sidelines of a game and wanting to join in, but not knowing how to because the rules or techniques are not clearly understood. For you as a tutor this represents a fairly low level of challenge because the learner is not intrinsically hostile to participating, they are just not clear on what they need to do. In this circumstance, modelling is a useful strategy. This may involve actually starting a piece of work for a learner while talking through what you are doing as you proceed. In this way, you are helping to clarify not only *what* the learners need to do, but also showing them *how* to approach the task. In many cases, getting started is the hardest part of any task and once learners are clear what is required, they should be able to continue with no more than the usual level of support. However, you will need to be careful, as some learners will try to persuade you to complete the work for them.

Reluctance to participate

This has many similarities with lack of understanding, but is accompanied with a degree of negative feeling about the actual learning process, materials or environment. It is this negativity that is preventing the learner from engaging. You need to explore with learners why they feel this way and what is acting as a barrier to their learning. Try to engage the learner in a conversation about the current difficulty. Provide time for the learner to talk about their feelings and be prepared to hear how little they enjoy the subject, the work, being with the other learners or whatever else they dislike. However, after you have given the learner an opportunity to share these views, move on to consider how this difficulty might be addressed. Use open questions like 'what are you finding particularly difficult?', 'where do you think you stopped understanding this process?' or 'if I organise the work in this way does it make it any easier to understand?' Once you have a firmer foundation to work from you will be more able to help the learner to engage and complete the work. Although the learner may still retain some residual negative feelings, being able to complete the work will allow the learner to experience some sense of success, which is likely to reduce their negative feelings.

Active resistance and hate

These two final configurations represent worst-case scenarios. In these examples learning has deteriorated to such an extent that learners openly express their loathing of college work and find ways to ensure they do not participate. You might find it difficult to imagine what circumstances could lead learners to become so hostile towards learning, and yet hate is often linked to, or preceded by, fear. Being frightened is like being backed into a corner with all the exits blocked. If these feelings escalate, learners may feel they have little to lose and might as well express their fear in any way they can. Wallace suggests a useful list of different aspects of education that learners might find fearful, including:

- *you (yes, you, you scary person, you!);*
- *being ridiculed by the group for appearing clever;*
- *being ridiculed by the group for appearing stupid;*
- *discovering they are 'not clever enough' to do the work;*
- *being ostracised by the group for breaking rank;*
- *failure;*
- *drawing any kind of attention to themselves in case they're asked to do something embarrassing, like read aloud (and remember that at certain ages just about everything seemed embarrassing).*

(Wallace, 2007, page 11)

Framed in this way, it is not so difficult to imagine how intimidating learning can be and the challenges it presents for some students. If learning is conceived of as an uncertain and threatening battleground it is easy to see how some students, over time, have grown to hate learning.

Hate is a powerful emotion and can be created by a range of factors. However, it is unlikely that the learner will hate everything about the session. Try to determine what specific aspects of a session might be causing difficulty. Consider the three equations below:

- Hate the work + hate the tutor = virtually no chance of learning occurring
- Hate the work + like the tutor = some chance of learning occurring
- Hate the tutor + like the work = some chance of learning occurring

Each of these combinations impedes learning in some way, but only one of these configurations is likely to bring a halt to learning. Tutors are key to the learning process and learning is most productive when students have positive feelings about both the work and the tutor. You cannot necessarily change others, or make learners like you, but you can manage your own behaviour and emotions to increase the possibility of learners being able to make progress in your sessions. If it appears that there may be personality issues between you and the learners, which are making it difficult for learners to work in your sessions, try the simple questionnaire in the Reflective Task below.

Of course, the ideal learning equation is 'Like the work + like the tutor'. If this can be achieved not only will learning definitely occur, but everyone involved in the learning equation will have enjoyed the process.

REFLECTIVE TASK

How learner-friendly are you as a tutor? Although this is a fun quiz and is not intended as a definitive assessment of your interactions with learners it will help you to gain an indication of your working relationships with students. It will also provide you with some interesting themes to reflect upon, and may help you identify areas for further professional development.

> Tutor/learner relationships quiz
> Indicate how strongly you agree with each of the following statements, where 5 = strongly agree and 1 = strongly disagree. If you are feeling adventurous you may wish to distribute this same questionnaire to a group of learners you teach to gauge how they feel about you and to see if they hold similar perceptions. However, if you choose to do this, you need to ensure learner anonymity.
> 1. I ensure that I find time to have a friendly word with each learner 1 2 3 4 5
> 2. I try to regularly use positive body language such as smiling, nodding, etc. 1 2 3 4 5
> 3. I know and correctly use each learner's name 1 2 3 4 5
> 4. I regularly use evidence-based praise 1 2 3 4 5
> 5. Learners feel enabled to ask questions openly in my sessions 1 2 3 4 5
> 6. Learners feel well supported in my classes 1 2 3 4 5
> 7. When managing poor behaviour I focus on actions rather than personalities 1 2 3 4 5
> 8. I apply agreed class rules consistently 1 2 3 4 5
> 9. I know something about my learners besides their academic ability 1 2 3 4 5
> 10. Learners seek me out to talk to me 1 2 3 4 5

Analysis

Over 45	You have strong positive relationships with your learners, who are well supported in your sessions. You enjoy being with learners and they enjoy being with you.
35-44	You work well with learners and they are comfortable in your presence. With a little more work these relationships could be even further improved.
25-34	You have the potential to work well with learners. However, there seems to be some sort of barrier that is preventing you from engaging more fully. Could you be personalising behavioural challenges?
16-24	You sometimes feel drained by teaching and wonder why your classes feel so dull and tiresome. Both you and your learners leave the sessions as quickly as you can.
Less than 15	You may wonder why you have come into teaching. You do not enjoy it and neither do your learners.

A final thought – while this may have appeared to be a light-hearted, possibly even childish exercise, it is important to remember that some learners need to have information packaged in novel ways to help them engage with learning. This quiz has served a dual function. It has provided an opportunity for you to reflect on your interpersonal skills and has given you a possible model that you could adapt to use in your own teaching.

Management by consent

FE is unlike any other sector in education. It neither screens by ability, as is the case with HE, nor has an entirely conscript population, as occurs in the statutory sector. FE prides itself on being able to provide a new and different offer to learners, which is not replicated elsewhere and willingly accepts learners of all abilities onto its programmes. Many learners who come to FE will have already experienced traditional approaches to classroom management and will be familiar with strict, teacher-centred styles of discipline. These traditional forms of class management do not rest easily in the FE sector and tutors need to explore other ways of working with learners.

It is important to remember that however you may wish to think of your learning environment you need to recognise there is a power balance within that environment. As an employee of the college, centre or unit where you work, you will have institutional power invested in you and, should you choose, the ability to exercise this power. Most learners are mindful of this dynamic and are aware that you have authority over them. Some learners are fearful of this and have come to view all authority figures as punishing and controlling. Although learners may not fear you as an individual, they certainly may fear what you have the ability to do. How you use this power, though, is a matter of choice – you can choose to autocratically retain sole control of power or may choose to democratically share power with learners.

This can be simply represented as follows:

Figure 5.2: Classroom management approaches.

If you choose to move away from traditionalism and adopt a more democratic style, you will need to develop strong interpersonal relationships with your learners, for it is through the strength and quality of these relationships that you will be able to manage the environment and to promote learning. In the sense that democracy is based on agreement and co-operation, by employing a democratic management style, you will now be managing by consent. And by extension of this logic, it is important to remember that any learning that takes place can only happen with the consent of your learners.

It is important to stress here that *management by consent is not the same as management by permission. Managers initially seek consent, but in the end, they alone have the authority to make decisions and will carry the accountability for that decision* (Freemantle, 1997, page 54). Although models from industry cannot be neatly superimposed onto education environments, there are existing parallels between this approach and the adult-centred teaching methods often promoted in colleges. College tutors often negotiate class rules with learners and seek to persuade them to accept collective responsibility for ensuring these rules are adhered to. 'Management' in this sense is not the imposition of some draconian code, but it is very much with the learners' permission. Management by consent is simply an extension of this approach.

REFLECTIVE TASK

What class management style do you believe you usually adopt? Do you encourage learners to share power and take collective responsibility in your sessions? Do your learners believe that you do this? Do you consider power sharing to be appropriate? Would this apply to all learning environments? Are there any learning environments where you believe this would be a wholly inappropriate strategy? What are the potential risks of power sharing? What are the possible benefits?

Working in partnership with schools

14–16-year-olds have different needs to the majority of college users. They are very much out of their usual environment and are expected to accommodate a different set of rules and working practices. While many 14–16-year-olds enjoy the opportunity of working in a new environment, they might, however, find this a disturbing experience and struggle to manage the increased freedom college allows. Some have developed an *uncool to work* (Jackson, 2006, page 74) attitude and do not want to *be seen to work hard* (*ibid*).Other learners will be disorientated by the size and unfamiliarity of the college and appear lost. Sometimes, these new challenges and changes can cause learners to act in a childish or juvenile way. Simply changing the venue where learners are studying is unlikely to produce an immediate positive effect on them.

Schools and the parents/guardians/carers of young people attending colleges should be made aware of the important differences between the two environments. It is particularly important that the families of young people appreciate that while students are in college they are not continually supervised, are very likely to mix with older learners and could come into contact with other members of the public while on college premises. If any of these factors presents a risk or gives rise to concern, then a decision would need to be made on the viability of the venture. At the core of this decision, the principles of ECM would need to be maintained, and the safety and well-being of young people should be protected at all times.

> **CASE STUDY**
> **IFP**
> You have arrived to teach your usual group and you notice that there is a room change notice on the door of the class next to yours. The usual IFP class that takes place in this room has been moved because of scheduled exams. You are not unduly concerned about this, because room changes happen regularly in college and you are quietly happy about this temporary arrangement, because the noise made by this group sometimes disturbs your session. However, shortly after your lesson has started, a flustered exam invigilator knocks on your door to ask you what to do. The room she was expecting to invigilate the exam in is now occupied by a class of 14-year-olds with their teacher from the local school. The invigilator has pointed out that the group should move to the alternative classroom to allow the exam to take place as arranged. The schoolteacher has refused, stating it is unsettling to move this group of learners.

Discussion

Imagine you are the college tutor that has been approached by the exam invigilator. What issues does this situation raise for you? Where do you believe your responsibilities lie? How would you work with the invigilator and the IFP schoolteacher? What should your immediate actions be? Would your actions be any different if the IFP group had, for convenience, simply moved into your class instead? Who needs to know that this event has taken place? What are the issues for future school/college liaison? Are there any staffing or rooming issues raised by this incident?

Risk assessments

Although students may attend college for part of their school week, as long as they remain on the school roll they are still the responsibility of the school. The *loco parentis* standing is not transferred to colleges, and while colleges are required to demonstrate a duty of care, the onus of responsibility remains with the school. Because of this relationship, colleges will need to work collaboratively with schools and *all* activities for younger learners should be properly risk assessed, *including* those which are classroom based. These assessments need to consider all aspects of the session including:

- resources, both human and physical;
- the environment;
- most significantly, the level of risk the learners themselves present.

If there is a likely risk of harm occurring to learners, staff or significant damage to property, then that activity should not be completed.

REFLECTIVE TASK

James, a construction lecturer, has been working with an IFP group from the local secondary school. He has 14 students in this group. He has been working on a project to build an outdoor adventure area for primary school-aged children. It is apparent that the learners have little real understanding of the materials that would be needed to construct such a play area and lack any concept of scale or quantities of materials that would be needed. To help them develop a better practical understanding, James would

the New Labour government, which appeared to positively endorse the idea of *institutional collaboration to deliver the 14–19 entitlement* (Hodgson and Spours, 2008, page 98). Adding further support to this idea, Ed Balls, the then-Secretary of State for Children, Schools and Families, publicly stated that *enthusiasm for collaborative working is one of the great strengths of our education system* (DCSF, 2008a, page 3), and he indicated that he saw this way of working as the way forward for both colleges and schools.

As education continues to evolve, partnership working provides a vehicle that can help address many of these needs and challenges education now faces. The following list represents some of the most pressing reasons which demand that colleges and schools enter into meaningful and productive collaborative working relationships to meet local and regional needs of 14–19-year-old learners:

- *To share resources and expertise* – Because of the way colleges and schools have developed historically, they often have very different physical resources, which may include large, specialised equipment such as vehicle maintenance bays or beauty salons. By the same token, they may also have developed the skills of their staff in different ways. These physical and human resources are usually locked into the employing establishment, and this has resulted in specific expertise and resources being tied to an individual college or school. This model is ill-equipped to meet learners' needs, who should have access to the best quality resources available in a locality. To enable effective utilisation of resources, colleges and schools need to reach agreement, which facilitates resources being shared across establishments.
- *To strengthen existing provision* – By sharing human and physical resources across providers, colleges and schools will have access to a pool of highly skilled and well-trained staff and the opportunity to make use of the best available equipment. Access to such high quality resources is likely to result in a corresponding improvement in the quality of courses and therefore enhance provision.
- *To provide relevant programmes of study* – While schools are still largely obliged to provide courses that meet the requirements of the National Curriculum, they can now offer programmes that traditionally have been the preserve of FE colleges. By sharing information gleaned from college and school students, local industry and other interest groups, providers will be able to develop suitable, relevant courses to meet the needs of the local population and industry. Further, although a single institution may struggle to achieve viable group numbers to offer a course, by bringing learners together from several establishments, it may be possible to provide a course which otherwise could not have been offered.
- *To re-establish a degree of local rationalisation of provision* – The Regional Development Agencies (RDAs) have been specifically tasked to ensure appropriate skills are developed within a geographical region. Post-1992, there was significant expansion of the FE sector, which created considerable overlap in provision. While this new open market approach to education may have improved consumer choice, it did not necessarily address the economic needs of an area. Although rationalisation of provision may not be desired by individual colleges, once colleges are returned to LA control there is likely to be an even greater emphasis on achieving this, so that the skills set of a region can be efficiently and effectively developed and unnecessary duplication can be avoided.

In addition to engaging in partnerships for the reasons identified above, the DCSF suggests that by entering into partnerships with schools, colleges will gain from the following benefits, which include:

- *supporting subject specialism and access to the 14–19 Diploma offer;*
- *sharing curricular expertise to raise standards in local schools, by supporting vocational learning programmes;*
- *spreading the values and ethos of further education to schools;*
- *promoting innovation in education;*

● *challenging and stretching schools' most able pupils through – for example – gifted and talented programmes and summer schools;*
● *providing continuing professional development opportunities for staff.*

(DSCF, 2008a, page 5)

As changes in education continue and accelerate, the need for partnership and multi-agency working has become increasingly apparent. Indeed, the advent of the Diplomas and a greater central government emphasis on improving the skills of the nation, whether in education or work, has virtually assured that this type of working arrangement will continue to grow and is likely to become the accepted way of working for most colleges and schools.

REFLECTIVE TASK

Consider the sorts of partnerships that are in place for your own institution. Which organisations and groups has your workplace chosen to work with? How long have these partnerships been running? What is the view among staff in relation to these partnerships? What benefits can you identify for this type of collaborative working? What issues, if any, has partnership working created for your college? How have these been addressed?

Building partnerships and working with schools

Many partnerships between colleges and schools have developed in an organic, ad-hoc fashion and were opportunistic in their beginning, rather than deliberate and strategic. While Chapter 5 considered some of the dilemmas that may arise as a consequence of having school-aged learners on college premises, this section will review the issues involved in forming effective and appropriately managed school partnerships.

Types of contact

There is no set defined model for setting up a working partnership with schools. Initial contact may be established as a result of proximity, mutual interest, by suggestion from the LA or because staff from each institution know each other. Any one of these approaches has the potential to be the start of a successful partnership. Equally, there are a variety of different types of contact that partners may wish to use once initial contact has been achieved. Table 6.1 describes the four main types of working arrangements in use between colleges and schools in the LLS sector. Although not exclusively, exchanges between colleges and schools are predominantly concerned with school students visiting college premises. However, it is possible for the exchange to occur in the other direction, and college students may visit schools for a variety of different reasons, such as mentoring school students and advising them of the opportunities available at college.

Managing the partnership

Once the partnership has been established, it will need to be managed and there will need to be an agreed set of terms and conditions by which the collaborating organisations operate. For a partnership to be successful, it will need the endorsement of the senior management teams of both establishments. Although informal contact may be possible for small-scale, short-term arrangements, it is not possible for a partnership to function effectively for any

Type of contact	Appropriate uses
One-off visits	This may be useful for some type of initial introductory contact for learners from schools. There is no expectation on the part of either establishment, or the visitors, that the contact will continue in a structured organised fashion beyond the single visit, although this is possible. It may form part of a school's careers programme or may be part of a college's marketing strategy. This sort of contact could also be used by college or school staff who wish to gain greater awareness of the operation of either institution, or to complete fact-finding investigations. It is usually easy to discontinue this sort of arrangement, as neither organisation has made a significant investment in an ongoing partnership.
Small-scale projects	This may be used to develop some particular aspect of the curriculum, for example to provide sports students a chance to develop their football coaching skills with secondary school students, over a fixed time span. Organisations may choose this sort of working arrangement as a result of limited resources, availability of staff or students, or other difficulties involved in maintaining more sustained contact. After the project has taken place, contact may lay dormant until the next occasion that another small-scale project needs to happen, or may be ended.
Occasional intermittent contact	This type of contact implies regular contact between the two organisations. Cycles of contact could be termly or for longer time periods. Contact is usually sustained in between meetings by telephone or email. This type of contact assumes a level of commitment on the part of both organisations involved, and indicates a wish to sustain relationships between organisations. This type of contact may be useful for longitudinal project work, or could be part of a carousel of activities where school students gain experience in a variety of different college departments.
Prolonged sustained contact	This model assumes regular contact over a significant period of time. It is indicative of a successfully established partnership, in which both organisations derive sufficient benefit to make a substantial investment in the relationship. This type of partnership is useful to help school students build up an ongoing relationship with their host college, and for colleges to engage in continuous recruitment from schools. In this arrangement, school students may visit colleges once a week or more for taught sessions, or staff from either institution may teach across sectors to provide seamless instruction.

Table 6.1: Types of working arrangements in use between colleges and schools in the LLS sector.

considerable time without the appropriate level of senior support. While such an agreement may not extend to being a formalised legally binding arrangement, it is important that there is some written documentation, which identifies how the partnership will work. Failure to have an agreed management strategy can result in friction between the collaborating organisations, and may ultimately cause the partnership to break down.

CASE STUDY
Developing links
Michelle had worked in a secondary school as a main scale drama teacher before taking up employment in a nearby FE college as course leader for drama in the Performing Arts Department. Although Michelle had transferred to another sector, she maintained contact with her colleagues at the school. Aware the college had better facilities than the

school, Michelle saw the opportunity to engage in cross-phase working, and organised a series of three sessions for Year 10 drama students to visit the college and take part in a joint improvisation with her BTEC National Performing Arts group. While this venture was very successful in terms of student satisfaction, with both college and school students identifying how much they had enjoyed the experience and how beneficial it had been to work with different staff and students, Michelle was advised by her Head of Department that such sorts of events were inappropriate.

Discussion

What issues does this case study raise about setting up partnership working? What general procedures or protocols would it have been advisable for Michelle to follow to avoid difficulty with her Head of Department? If formal procedures were not in place, what general approach do you think it would have been prudent to adopt? What questions for partnership working has this particular venture raised for future collaborative working? Are there any issues about bringing groups of different ages together in this way? How could an exchange of this type be organised more successfully?

Operational concerns

Once a partnership has been established, it is important that there is agreement on operational matters. To ensure that the partnership runs smoothly, organisations will need to ensure that they have addressed the following issues:

- *Identifying staff involved in the partnership and communication channels* – This will need to be specified on at least two levels. Firstly, the senior managers from both organisations need to be identified. Such information is required if the terms of the partnership need to be changed at any stage. Secondly, the staff who will be involved in the day-to-day running and delivery of the programme need to be confirmed. It is likely that the staff involved in the day-to-day running of the partnership will handle any immediate concerns that arise and will manage minor presenting issues. Naming staff in this way facilitates communication and allows matters to be dealt with swiftly and efficiently.
- *Specifying communication channels* – A strategy for communication, which identifies how communication will be conducted, needs to be agreed. This strategy should stipulate the frequency of contact, who is responsible for maintaining contact between the organisations and how information will be disseminated across the organisation. Specifying the terms under which contact occurs reduces the likelihood of misunderstanding between organisations.
- *Agreeing discipline responsibilities* – It is likely at some stage both college and school staff will need to deal with discipline issues. It is important that both organisations have a clear understanding of how this will be managed and who should take primary responsibility for the concern. For example, if a college student insults a member of a school party, is this a college or a school matter? Alternatively, if a school student damages college property, who should deal with this? Often, agreements specify that whichever member of staff arrives at an incident first manages the situation in a proportionate way, but the issue is then referred back to the home institution of the students involved, and feeds into the mainstream policy on managing behaviour. Clear documentation of any incident will need to be kept and shared with relevant personnel.
- *Staff roles* – It needs to be clear which staff fulfil which functions. Who will do teaching? Who will carry out pastoral work? What other staff can participants expect to have contact with (e.g. administrators, library staff, refectory staff)? Who will take primary responsibility for preparing written reports on students? Will staff involved in teaching be expected to attend pastoral and progress reporting events at either institution? There is no single defined model used here, but for the partnership to be effective and successful, staff roles will need to be agreed between the co-operating institutions.

not necessarily equip them for more highly skilled positions in many forms of employment and, more often than not, the majority of job opportunities available for 14–19-year-olds are more likely to need level 2 type qualifications.

Further, the skills identified by the LSC as desirable for graduate employees, *bear only a weak relationship with formal certification and lie outside the spectrum of skill that qualifications assess* (Pring *et al.*, 2009, page 142). In essence, it appears the skills many employers seek are not directly linked to qualifications and are more concerned with personal attributes and disposition. If the skills identified by the LSC are truly what employers are looking for, then it would be unreasonable to suggest that education was solely responsible for not meeting the needs of employment.

A further difficult and unresolved conundrum when considering the needs of employers is that sometimes companies may wish to mould new staff into certain ways of thinking or working. While such an approach is not necessarily at odds with employing staff with higher level qualifications, it may be advantageous to employ staff who have been less exposed to different views, as they could be more willing to accept preferred company practices.

However, industry has consistently shown that it *value(s) various key and generic skills* (LSC, 2007, page 10) and it is likely *there will be a continuation of the recent significant increases in the overall demand for skills* (LSC, 2007, page 11). In particular, employers *place considerable emphasis upon skills such as communication, IT, team working, problem-solving* (LSC, 2007, page 61) and in some cases appear to value these skills above *formal qualifications* (ibid). If any charge can be levelled against education for not meeting employers' needs, it is that education has not supplied a sufficient pool of young people who have adequately developed key skills.

CASE STUDY

Neil

Neil owns and manages a small catering business. As a result of increasing workload he now needs to take on another employee. However, this has not been as simple as Neil imagined. Below is Neil's account of this experience:

As a young person, I had struggled a bit at school. After a long time I managed to set up my own small catering business, with a shop outlet and providing hot and cold lunches for events. I had to go back to college to get my NVQs in catering, learn to do my books and things like that, but I was then able to apply for a loan and set my business up. I now have four other people working for me. I really wanted to help another person into work, because I know how hard it can be to get a job. I contacted the job centre and they sent me round Simon, a 19-year-old, who had left school at 16 without any qualifications and been doing a variety of short-term casual jobs in retail and catering, but had been out of work for the last seven months. He seemed nice enough, but when I talked to him about doing a catering NVQ with me he wasn't at all keen. What's more his maths was very weak and when I suggested he go back to college in the evening (like I had) to try and pick up some qualifications, again, he didn't seem interested. As a small business owner, I have to keep a careful watch on materials, as I run very slim profit margins, and if materials are wasted, I could easily start to fall into debt. I need all of my staff to be properly trained, and to understand how to measure, weigh and calculate the ingredients they need accurately, so that I can minimise waste, maximise profit and stay in business.

Discussion

What do you believe are the employer's responsibilities in terms of training this new employee? Should the employer take more of an active interest in helping Simon improve his basic skills? What initiatives or support are you aware of that might assist the employer in training Simon? What support could Simon access independently to help him develop his skills?

UK competitiveness in a European and global market

The pace of change in employment has accelerated and this trend is likely to continue. In 2009, the DCSF reported that:

- *by 2020 there will be 5 million fewer low skilled jobs in Britain;*
- *40% of all jobs in 2020 will require a graduate qualification;*
- *today's learners will have 10–14 jobs by age 38;*
- *we are currently preparing students for jobs that don't yet exist.*

(Adapted from DCSF, 2009, page 1)

The UK needs to be able to respond to this environment and to equip learners for the challenges they are likely to face in a rapidly changing world. While it is problematic to obtain reliable international information, data indicates that *England lies behind* (LSDA, 2005, page 32) other developed economies, including Australia and Denmark, both in terms of achievement of learners and numbers of students enrolled in study at levels 2, 3 and higher level qualifications. Further, it appears that the UK is ill equipped to respond to the changing economic climate likely to prevail in the twenty-first century and beyond.

In order to provide and sustain economic prosperity, to meet the employment demands of the home market and to compete effectively both in Europe and with other economies, Leitch identified that there needs to be a *new national ambition for the UK to be a world leader in skills* (2006, page 55). Unless the UK can achieve this ambition it *will remain average by international standards*(ibid), and can expect to be overtaken by other European and emerging economies. To achieve this new ambition, the UK needs to ensure that it has an appropriately skilled population so that it can compete with other economies. In practice, this will mean that by 2020 the UK needs to ensure that:

- 95 per cent of adults have the basic skills of functional literacy and numeracy;
- over 90 per cent of adults are qualified to at least level 2;
- it shifts the balance of intermediate skills to level 3;
- over 40 per cent of adults are qualified to level 4 and above.

(Adapted from Leitch, 2006, page 55)

This is an ambitious target and to achieve this goal, Leitch recommended that the necessary investment needed *must be shared between the Government, individuals and employers* (2006, page 58). Because skills for the future cannot be entirely predicted, colleges and employers will need to be responsive to an ever-changing environment, and to fill skills gaps that might emerge. Both colleges and employers, through initiatives such as Train to Gain, have demonstrated their capacity to tackle skills shortages, and such flexibility will need to continue into the future.

Who are the principal employers in your area? What are the skills needed by these employers? Have the skills needed by employers in your region changed over the last five or ten years? Are there any new or emerging employers within your area? What skills do these employers require employees to have? What has been the impact of other international competitors on employment in your region?

The emergence of the NEET population

One group that has received much media attention is young people who are Not in Education, Employment or Training (NEET). The New Labour government recognised that *engagement in learning and educational attainment are critical if young people are to make a success of their lives* (DCSF, 2008b, page i), and to later be in a position to enter employment. While there has always been a proportion of young people who have either been economically inactive or not involved in some form of training, worryingly, the *'NEET' rate has hovered at an average of about 10% for 16-18 year olds* (Hayward *et al.*, 2008, page 11) since the late 1980s. Although it would be inaccurate to describe this population as a homogenous group, and there is significant diversity within this group, they appear to share a common experience of low academic achievement, failure to engage with the statutory education system and social and economic disadvantage. NEET learners are of further interest to the government, as they at particular risk of becoming drawn into *gang membership and involvement in crime (ibid*, page 24).

These cycles of underachievement and disadvantage appear to replicate themselves so that whole families (and sometimes large portions of communities) appear to develop a habit of worklessness, and, over time, become unemployable. By not being productively engaged, it is estimated that each new NEET will cost taxpayers an average of £97,000 during their lifetime through lost revenue and benefit payments and at worst can cost more than £300,000 apiece (BBC News, 2006).

The Labour government, determined to address this difficult and challenging issue, responded by introducing a package of measures designed to encourage and promote participation amongst the NEET population. While these steps were not exclusively for the benefit of NEET learners, they were a principal target audience. Specific measures taken included:

- nationally launching The Educational Maintenance Allowance (EMA) in 2004, a means-tested grant, that was available to all 16-year-olds to help young people to remain in education (the Coalition government has announced the EMA will be scrapped from 2011);
- making Entry to Employment (E2E) programmes leading to an apprenticeship, employment or further learning widely available for 16–18-year-olds not currently engaging in any form of post-compulsory learning;
- from 2009, introducing the Foundation Learning Tier, a coherent national suite of qualifications and training available at pre-entry, entry and level 1, which include GCSEs, Diplomas and vocational qualifications enabling *all* learners to progress within the national qualifications and credit framework.

The government further intends to address its concerns regarding NEET students and general low participation rates in education in the UK, and has committed to raising the school leaving age, so that by 2013 all 17-year-olds, and by 2015 all 18-year-olds will need to be either in education, training or work.

To assist colleges and schools in their efforts to support young people and to re-engage NEET learners, in 2001 the government established the Connexions service. Connexions *has a broad remit . . . to provide integrated information, advice and guidance (IAG) and access to personal development opportunities for all 13–19 year olds in England* (LSC, 2003, page 7) and was charged *to end current fragmentation of services* by ensuring *all the needs of a young person were met in an integrated and coherent manner* (DfEE, 2000, page 35). To achieve this, all young people within this age range were given access to a personal advisor, who was responsible for providing relevant advice at key junctions in a young person's life so that they could *make a successful transition to further education, employment and adult life* (*ibid*, page 36). Personal advisors were to be readily accessible to young people and were consequently based in colleges, schools, youth offending teams (YOTs), social services departments and in community and voluntary provision to work directly alongside lecturers, teachers and other staff employed by the host organisation.

PRACTICAL TASK PRACTICAL TASK **PRACTICAL TASK** PRACTICAL TASK **PRACTICAL TASK**

Find out how your college works with the Connexions service. Are there personal advisors based within your college or do they work from a centralised base serving a number of organisations? What sorts of students do they work with? What sorts of services do they provide? What is the perception of the usefulness of the Connexions service by the staff in your organisation? How does this perception align with that of the young people who Connexions support? What have been the positive benefits of the Connexions service to your organisation and the young people they work with? In your assessment, has Connexions been successful in providing a 'one-stop-information-service' for young people?

The role of *Every Child Matters*

Every Child Matters (ECM) is a government initiative designed to promote the interests and safety of infants, children and young people up to age 19, established as a result of the multiple failures of different organisations *to intervene appropriately in order to protect* (Barker, 2009, page 9) a child from harm, resulting in eventual death. ECM is a *restructuring of children's services, including education, child protection, health and the Youth Criminal Justice system to ensure all these services are working together to provide a multi-agency approach* (Knowles, 2009, page 1) to make certain the needs of all children are met in a timely and effective manner. The ECM agenda endeavours to guarantee that each child and young person is given the necessary support to:

- be healthy;
- stay safe;
- enjoy and achieve;
- make a positive contribution;
- achieve economic well-being.

By passing the Children's Act in 2004, the government supplied the legislative framework needed to implement the five key aims of ECM. Colleges and schools are not capable of meeting the five key aims of ECM by themselves and the multi-agency approach demanded by ECM means that colleges and schools have been obliged to work with professionals from an increasing network of organisations such as healthcare professionals, social workers and representatives of the criminal justice system including youth offending teams and the police. For some colleges and schools, this has simply meant an extension of existing good practice, but for others this has required finding new ways of working collaboratively with other professionals outside of their immediate environment for the common good of the children and young people in their care.

REFLECTIVE TASK

How well do you understand the implications of the ECM agenda and the Children Act? How has your college or school prepared to ensure they can implement the five key aims of ECM? Which agencies are your college or school working with to support them in implementing these key aims? Have there been any changes to the numbers or types of organisations your institution is now working with? Who are the key personnel in your establishment tasked with ensuring that ECM is fully embedded?

A SUMMARY OF **KEY POINTS**

In the past, colleges and schools operated in a far more autonomous fashion. They had a defined understanding of which programmes they could offer and who they needed to report success (or otherwise) to. Lines of responsibility and accountability were narrowly defined, and educational providers were responsible for specific contributions to a child or young person's experience. However, this is a description of the past. Colleges and schools are no longer solely and exclusively responsible for meeting the educational needs of young people and their roles have changed and expanded. Colleges and schools are now part of a much wider network, in which all agencies, under the unifying umbrella of ECM, are expected to work together to meet the needs of children and young people.

This chapter has explored:

> **the roles of colleges and schools in the wider community;**

> **the need to form partnerships between colleges and schools;**

> **the features of partnership working of colleges and schools;**

> **the needs of industry and employers;**

> **UK competitiveness in a European and global market;**

> **the emergence and impact of the NEET population on education;**

> **the significance of ECM in meeting young people's needs.**

REFERENCES REFERENCES REFERENCES REFERENCES REFERENCES REFERENCES

Barker, R (2009) Background to Understand Every Child Matters, in Barker, R (ed) *Making Sense of Every Child Matters, Multi-professional Practice Guidance.* Bristol: The Policy Press.

BBC (2006) *Meet the Neets.* Available online at *www.bbc.co.uk/go/pr/fr/-/1/hi/programmes/politics_show/6160751.stm*

DCSF (2008a) *Academies and Trusts: Opportunities for Schools, Sixth-form and FE Colleges.* Nottingham: DCSF.

DCSF (2008b) *Reducing the Number of Young People not in Education, Employment, or Training (NEET).* Nottingham: DCSF.

DCSF (2009) *14–19 Briefing: Making Change Happen.* London: HMSO.

DfEE (2000) *Connexions – The Best Start in Life for Every Young Person.* Nottingham: DfEE.

Hayward, G, Wilde, S and Williams, R (2008) *Rathbone/Nuffield Review Engaging Youth Enquiry.* Available online at *www.nuffield14-19review.org.uk*

Hodgson, A and Spours, K (2008) *Education and Training 14–19 – Curriculum, Qualifications and Organisation.* London: Sage.

Knowles, G (2009) *Ensuring Every Child Matters.* London: Sage.

Learning and Skills Council (2003) *Working Together – Connexions and Adult Information, Advice and Guidance Partnerships.* Coventry: LSC.

Learning and Skills Council (2007) *Skills in England 2003, Volume 2, Research Report.* Coventry: LSC.

Leitch, S (2006) *Prosperity for All in the Global Economy – World Class Skills.* London: The Stationery Office.

LSDA (2005) *Can We Compare Post-16 Performance With the 'Best in the World': An Empirical Assessment.* Shaftesbury: LSDA.

Pring, R, Hayward, G, Hodgson, A, Johnson, J, Keep, E, Oancea, A, Rees, G, Spours, K and Wilde, S (2009) *Education For All – The Future of Education and Training for 14–19 Year Olds.* London: Routledge.

FURTHER READING FURTHER READING **FURTHER READING** FURTHER READING

Ofsted (2000) *New Start Partnership Projects for 14–16 Year Olds in Schools 1997–1999.* London: Ofsted.

Ofsted (2005) *Increased Flexibility Programme at Key Stage 4.* London: Ofsted.

Ofsted and FEFC (1999) *Post-16 Collaboration – School Sixth Form and the Further Education Sector.* Coventry: FEFC.

Websites

www.british.council.org/eumd-partnership-fe-strategy.htm

www.excwllwncwgateway.org.uk/pdf/Reaching-further.pdf

www.teachernet.gov.uk/wholeschool/behaviour/sspg/

7
Conclusion

The objectives of this chapter

This chapter provides a summary of the key issues raised in the book and offers suggestions for further reading. In doing this, it provides further support for you to meet the LLUK Standards listed at the beginning of each of the earlier chapters, and, in addition, the following Standards:

- **Equality, diversity and inclusion in relation to learners, the workforce, and the community (AK3.1; AP3.1).**
- **Reflection and evaluation of their own practice and their continuing professional development as teachers (AK4.3; AP4.1; AP4.2; AP4.3).**
- **Collaboration with other individuals, groups and/or organisations with a legitimate interest in the progress and development of learners (AK5.1; AP5.1).**

14–19 context

This book has explored the development of the 14–19 agenda, from the early introduction of general vocational courses into schools and colleges as part of the 'new vocationalism' of the 1980s. It was the introduction of such programmes, ostensibly to provide education and training for the mass of young unemployed at the time, that led to suggestions that vocational education was directed at certain groups of working-class young people. This re-ignited the parity of esteem debate, and concerns that young people were being educated for different purposes according to their social class. These concerns have continued parallel with the development of the 14–19 agenda, and many of the policy initiatives which have led to the current position have been justified as being designed to address issues of parity of esteem as well as to meet the economic need for *world class skills* (Leitch, 2006, page 5). It is these economic imperatives, which, since the 1970s, have driven educational reforms such as the introduction of NVQs and GNVQs, the withdrawal of GNVQs, the short-lived Curriculum 2000 initiative, and the introduction of the Diploma. The issues that have arisen as a consequence of this are manifold, and so are alluded to in the context of other discussions – for example, in later discussions about the Diploma as well as in the discussion around collaborative and partnership working.

The Diploma: origins and implementation

Key aspects of the Diploma are the economic imperatives and employers' demands which have helped to shape it. The economic imperative is the need to be competitive within a globalised economy, which is seeing the emergence of countries such as India and China as powerful economic forces with the potential to contribute to the marginalisation of the UK on the world economic stage. These economic changes are occurring at the same time as our use of technology is increasing, leading to a demand for more highly qualified workers in order to enable the UK to compete effectively in this global environment.

Parallel with this have come vocal demands from employers for employees with the skills that industry needs – although it is not always clear what these are, nor the level of education required to enter different parts of the workforce. It is clear, however, that industry's require-ments will not be the same for all parts of the workforce. While the government has maintained its aim for all workers to be educated at least to level 2 in literacy, numeracy and ICT, for *some jobs an aptitude for particular types of work* is necessary, *or higher* level *qualifications such as a degree.* The introduction of the Diploma was an attempt to meet these needs, and to address concerns about the existing 14–19 curriculum and issues around parity of esteem of different educational routes.

Employers were involved in the development of the Diploma, and the work experience element is intended to relate it closely to the needs of industry. The structure is intended to provide a coherent framework, which will enable young people to pursue their ambitions to work in a particular area. However, take-up of the award has been limited, with many organisa-tions preferring to continue offering 'tried and tested' awards such as BTEC. Further, many academics have raised concerns about the new system, criticising it for attempting to be all things to all people – an inclusive qualification which meets the needs of students with learning difficulties operating at the lowest point of the mainstream framework, and those young people who intend to progress to university. Concerns around parity of esteem do not appear to have been addressed and there is little current research to demonstrate how successful the award is in preparing young people for work, meeting the needs of employers, providing an inclusive qualifications framework and meeting the needs of the whole spectrum of 14–19 ability. However, with such ambitious aims, it seems unlikely that all will be met in full.

Part of the reason for low take-up of the award may have been Conservative and Liberal criticisms of the Diploma. However, shortly after the 2010 general election the incoming Coalition government announced that the award would remain in place, as the government *want(ed) to see how the Diplomas work* (Gibb, June 2010). The Extended (or Academic) Diploma, was, however withdrawn in the same announcement. This effectively means that the current qualifications system is virtually unchanged from that of the early 1990s, as shown in Table 7.1 below.

1990s		2009 onwards	
Vocational	Academic	Vocational	Academic
GNVQs BTECs	GSCEs A levels	Diplomas BTECs	GCSEs A levels

Table 7.1: Comparison of qualifications from 1990s and 2009 onwards.

In the 1990s the vocational qualifications included the key skills components of numeracy, literacy and ICT. The contemporary Diploma similarly includes the functional skills compo-nent, which encompasses English, maths and ICT.

Implementing the Diploma

What has changed significantly since the early 1990s, and what may influence the outcome for the Diploma and vocational education more broadly, has been the development of partnership working in recent years. Although partnerships have been encouraged by government initiatives and policy, many evolved and made significant developments in advance of policy as they responded proactively to the early reports of the Tomlinson Committee. In some areas, partnerships were prepared for the full implementation of the

Tomlinson recommendations and effective partnerships and common timetables had been established. In other areas, work had been undertaken with bodies responsible for public transport to facilitate the movement of young people between sites. Where such effective partnerships have been established (and this is not consistent across the country) they have continued working together for the benefit of young people, and many have become more formal collaborations to support the implementation of the Diploma. These partnerships have also invested heavily in the Diploma, in terms of providing appropriate facilities for 14–16 students, and those following courses requiring specialist equipment such as Hair and Beauty or construction, to study in. It seems likely that this model of delivery will continue. Given the cost of the implementation of the Diploma, and the potential cost of rebranding it or introducing a new system, it also seems likely that it will remain in place for the foreseeable future, particularly given that any future developments will have to be undertaken in the context of difficult economic circumstances. Thus, any major changes to the 14–19 curriculum may be more likely to involve the academic, rather than the vocational curriculum.

International Baccalaureate, A* A levels and iGCSE

Some such changes have already been announced. In June 2010 the Coalition government reversed earlier policy around the iGCSE and International Baccalaureate, allowing head teachers to choose which qualifications to offer at their school. Criticisms of 'dumbing down' at both GCSE and A level (particularly in science and maths) led OfQual to suggest that new proposals to strengthen the content of these GCSEs were not sufficiently robust and some schools began to investigate the possibility of offering alternative qualifications. Many independent schools, which are not bound by government regulation in the same way as state schools, have already introduced alternative qualifications such as the iGCSE. It is likely that the schools opting for these alternatives will be those with a strong academic background and a largely middle-class, affluent intake who are destined for university and beyond. Critics of this approach argue that it will create a more advantaged tier of young people in the education system, who will be better able to access elite courses at elite institutions, leading to an even more divided education system and increasing the issues around parity of esteem.

An additional change (the introduction of the A* A level) has been subject to similar criticism. While many universities believe that it will help them to identify the brightest of the increasing numbers of candidates who hold three or more A grade A levels, critics argue that young people from less advantaged backgrounds, who have not attended schools with high achieving sixth forms, may have greater potential to achieve at university even if they have lower A level grades. Some critics fear that an A* grade could further disadvantage this group of young people, and reverse some of the progress made in recent years by widening participation initiatives. Since these announcements are so recent, it is not possible to suggest what the actual outcomes will be with any degree of certainty. While take-up of the Baccalaureate and iGCSE is influenced by universities (the success or otherwise of any qualification depends to a certain extent on the value that universities place on it in terms of access), this influence could increase in the near future as limits have been placed on university places. Consequently, securing a place at university is likely to become increasingly competitive, and schools and colleges are likely to explore ways of giving their students an 'edge' in the applications process. This may mean that some schools introduce alternative forms of assessment, such as iGCSE or Baccalaureate, if universities appear to be placing a higher value on these qualifications rather than standard qualifications such as GCSE or A level.

Consider the recent government policy announcements in respect of the Diploma, A level, iGCSE and Baccalaureate outlined above. You could also return to the earlier chapters, which discuss these issues in more detail. Think about the arguments for and against each of the changes and answer the following questions in respect of each qualification.

- Which arguments do you support?
- Why do you support it?
- What evidence or reading can you draw on to support your own thinking about each issue?

Achievement routes

One feature of an increase in the numbers of schools offering iGCSEs and the Baccalaureate would be greater complexity in the achievement framework, which is already very complicated (please see Chapter 3). Broadly speaking, there are three routes that young people can follow during the 14–16 stage, which are:

- Foundation Learning Tier;
- broad vocational route (e.g. BTEC or Diploma);
- academic route (GCSEs).

These routes become more extensive, and complicated, in the 16–19 phase, primarily because a young person can leave school at 16 and enter employment. This will continue to be the case after the school leaving age is raised to 18, providing the job has training included. During the 16–19 phase young people can choose to follow one of the five routes below.

- Foundation Learning Tier.
- Broad vocational route (e.g. BTEC or Diploma).
- Occupational route (NVQs, sometimes through an apprenticeship or with employment).
- Academic route (A levels).
- Alternative route.

In addition to these routes there is a raft of short course accreditation, providing qualifications such as OCNs, short course GCSEs and ASDAN awards. These are often referred to as the 'alternative' post-16 route, as these awards tend to have different uses for the 14–16 phase and 16–19 phase. Pre-16, short course GCSEs and other accreditation such as ASDAN are used to provide breadth to the curriculum and to recognise achievement in an area of the curriculum such as citizenship, which is mandatory but not always examined. For 14–16-year-olds, therefore, these qualifications are mostly part of mainstream provision. Post-16 short courses such as OCN and ASDAN awards are more often used to acknowledge learning in informal and alternative contexts, and as a means of widening participation and supporting people to re-engage with education. Such qualifications are often used on programmes and initiatives to support NEET young people to re-engage with education, as well as in community settings.

It is clear the achievement framework is complex even at face value, and the different exchange value of each credential makes this framework even more complicated. As

Ask a small group of your youngest learners what their career aim is. For five of them, draw out the range of possible trajectories that would enable them to achieve this aim. This might involve variously doing GCSEs, Diplomas, apprenticeships, A levels, NVQs or going to university. When you have completed your 'maps', see how many possible variations there are for each young person. Is there a benefit to any individual to pursue one or other of the routes you have mapped out? What is the benefit? When you have considered this, ask your students to create their own 'maps', and then spend some time going through them together as a group. Use this time to find out how many of the different options they were aware of. Did they come up with as many (or more) possibilities than you? Which route do they think is the 'best' and why? Do their views correspond with yours? Finally, what did you learn about the complexity of 14–19 education and the qualifications framework, and the understandings of your learners about both of these from this exercise?

NEETs

One of the groups who is, perhaps, most likely to have difficulty navigating their way through the 14–19 phase is those who are described as NEET. Despite government initiatives to reduce the numbers of young people who are not in education, employment or training, which include the introduction of the EMA, the new Foundation Learning Tier and E2E programmes, as well as the yet to be implemented raising of the school leaving age to 18, the numbers of young people classified as NEET has changed very little. One of the difficulties of working with this group is that they are often transient, difficult to pin down and it easy for them to be lost in the system. Some of these young people become engaged in criminality or gang membership, while others move on to benefits dependency or into education or employment. Thus, while many of the NEET group have characteristics in common, such as low achievement and poor educational experience, they are also a very diverse group. This is illustrated in the case studies below.

CASE STUDY
Megan and Corey
Megan was the sole carer for her terminally ill mother. She achieved five grade E/F GCSEs at 16+ and progressed to a level 1 course at a local college. Her attendance was intermittent and she was unclassified at the end of the year. Megan did not return to college but continued caring for her mother. Following her mother's death 18 months later, Megan was re-housed by the local authority and moved to a different part of town. Her social worker referred her to Connexions, which set up a number of places on courses at college and training providers. However, Megan only ever attended for a few weeks and then stopped going. She would then tell the careers advisor that she did not like the people there, or that they had been unkind to her. Megan became pregnant at 19, following which she claimed benefit and stayed at home to care for her baby.

Corey began skipping school when he was 13. He had very poor literacy skills and could not cope with the demands school placed on him. His mother and her partner, preoccupied with their own abusive and deteriorating relationship, did not notice. While wandering the streets he became involved with some youths who belonged to a local gang and made money by doing 'jobs' for more senior gang members. At 15, he was arrested in possession of heroin, which he was carrying for his own use. At this point, his mother threw him out, and he slept rough or on friends' floors. Corey did not turn up for his exams and had less than 30 per cent attendance for that year. At this point, his mother, the Careers service and social workers all lost contact with him. He was fined for being in possession of drugs and subsequently did not come to the attention of the authorities until he was arrested again, a few months later, after being involved in a gang fight during which a young man had died. He was sentenced to two years in a Young Offenders Institution for his part in this.

Discussion

Now consider...What similarities and differences are there between Megan and Corey? How might each of them be supported to engage with education and training? What specific support could have made a difference to either of them? To what extent do they have social problems and to what extent do they have educational problems? Can (and should) these be considered separately?

Every Child Matters

The Every Child Matters agenda is an over-arching policy, which, in theory at least, might have provided frameworks to support Megan and Corey. The five outcomes, discussed in detail in Chapter 6, are now embedded in the curriculum in a number of different ways, and it is the responsibility of all professionals working with children and young people to promote the outcomes for each individual they have responsibility for. The five outcomes are:

1. be healthy;
2. stay safe;
3. enjoy and achieve;
4. make a positive contribution;
5. achieve economic well-being.

Outcomes one, two and four are now embedded in the PSHE and citizenship curricula, and outcomes three, four and five are the natural outcomes of an effective education 14–19, which facilitates a young person to move into either HE or employment of their choice. The implementation of the ECM agenda has provided another imperative for partnership working, since a single young person (such as Corey) might have involvement with, for example, the education system, social services, the criminal justice system and the health service. Chapter 6 has illustrated how, through professionals working collaboratively, an integrated and more effective service can be put in place for those individuals who are in need of support. This issue of collaboration has, together with the diversity of the 14–19 agenda, formed a key theme of this book.

Conclusion

In conclusion, this book has covered a wide range of issues, exploring the history of the 14–19 agenda, the contemporary context of 14–19 education, including curriculum reform and achievement frameworks and pathways. It has explored teaching and behaviour management in a 14–19 context, making specific reference to some of the more challenging and disadvantaged groups of young people you may come across while teaching this age group. We have discussed many of the more contentious issues around 14–19, such as debates around parity of esteem and maintaining 'gold standard' A levels and GCSEs. Running throughout these diverse subjects and debates has been the notion of education communities, which have developed largely in response to the 14–19 agenda, though also, to an extent, in response to the imperatives of ECM. This may be seen as one of two key themes running through this book. The second is the complexity and diversity of the sector, the students making a transition through the 14–19 phase, and the professionals who work within it. It is this diversity of people, which, to a large extent, is responsible for the dynamism and enthusiasm which may be found in all settings in the sector and which make it such a rewarding area to work in.

A SUMMARY OF **KEY POINTS**

We hope that the book has developed your understanding of 14–19 education as we continue to move forward in an ever-changing policy arena, and conclude with a list of further reading that will help you to continue your professional development in this area.

This book has explored:

> the context of 14–19 education;

> the imperative for curriculum reform;

> current achievement routes and frameworks;

> education communities;

> teaching in a 14–19 context;

> managing behaviour in a 14–19 context;

> the emergence of an educational underclass and the NEET population.

REFERENCES REFERENCES REFERENCES **REFERENCES** REFERENCES REFERENCES

DfES (2005) *14–19 Education and Skills.* Annesley: DfES Publications.

Leitch, S (2006) *Prosperity for All in the Global Economy – World Class Skills.* London: The Stationery Office.

Working Group on 14–19 Reform (2004b) *14–19 Curriculum and Qualifications Reform Final Report of the Working Group on 14–19 Reform*. London: DfES.

FURTHER READING FURTHER READING **FURTHER READING** FURTHER READING

The further reading section of this final chapter is designed to support you to continue developing your knowledge and understanding of the 14–19 sector. It includes the most recent White Paper – reading the executive summary of this will give you a good overview to start with. You should also access and read each new policy as it is announced – this will help you to understand the reasoning behind local and national developments, and in turn, to explain these to your students. Up-to-date announcements can be found on the Department for Education website (address given below) and you can arrange to have regular updates emailed to you if you wish. Three of the texts listed relate directly to 14–19 education, but explore different aspects of the 14–19 context: Pring *et al*. report on the Nuffield 14-19 Review, Lumby and Foskett explore wider issues of policy, the curriculum and support, Hodgson and Spours critique the Diploma and Atkins explores the students' experiences of the 14–19 agenda.

Tomlinson provides a theoretical and political overview of education, which will be particularly helpful if you intend to go on to further study. The remaining texts, while written about lifelong learning rather than 14–19, include chapters on 14–19 issues or discuss broader concerns such as the curriculum, which, while including examples drawn from a wider context, are relevant to professionals working in the 14–19 sector. Finally, the websites listed will take you to the most current writing and research in this area, and you will find that the papers are freely available to download.

Atkins, L (2009) *Invisible Students, Impossible Dreams: Experiencing Vocational Education 14–19.* Stoke-on Trent: Trentham Books.

DfES (2005) *14–19 Education and Skills.* London: HMSO. Available online at *www.dfes.gov.uk/ publications/14-19educationandskills*

Hodgson, A and Spours, K (2007) Specialised Diplomas: Transforming the 14–19 Landscape in England? *Journal of Education Policy*, 22 (6): 657–73.

Lumby, J and Foskett, N (2005) *14–19 Education: Policy, Leadership and Learning.* London: Sage.

Pring, R *et al.* (2009) *Education for All: The Future of Education and Training for 14–19 Year Olds.* London: Routledge.

Tomlinson, S (2005) *Education in a Post-welfare Society (2nd ed).* Maidenhead: Open University Press.

Tummons, J (2009) *Curriculum Studies in the Lifelong Learning Sector.* Exeter: Learning Matters.

Wallace, S (2007) *Teaching, Tutoring and Training in the Lifelong Learning Sector (3rd ed).* Exeter: Learning Matters.

Wallace, S (2009) (Ed) *The Lifelong Learning Sector: Reflective Reader.* Exeter: Learning Matters.

Websites

www.data-archive.ac.uk/findingData/snDescription.asp?sn=3109

www.education.gov.uk/

www.nuffield14-19review.org.uk

www.tlrp.org/proj/index.html

Index

Added to a page number 'f' denotes a figure and 't' denotes a table.